Jesse Stuart

For Fred Eckman,
distinguished by
a Noon-Day Devil.

Jesse Stuart

Kentucky's Chronicler-Poet

J. R. LeMaster

Memphis State University Press

Manufactured in the United States of America

INTERNATIONAL STANDARD BOOK NUMBER 0-87870-049-8

Library of Congress Cataloging in Publication Data

LeMaster, J   R   1934-
    Jesse Stuart, Kentucky's chronicler-poet.

    Bibliography: p.
    Includes index.
    1.   Stuart, Jesse, 1907-   —Criticism and interpretation.
    I.   Title.
PS3537.T92516Z76   811'.52   79-28224
    ISBN 0-87870-049-8

Acknowledgements

Some of the material in *Jesse Stuart: Kentucky's Chronicler-Poet* first appeared in somewhat revised form as "Jesse Stuart: Kentucky's Chronicler-Poet," Ph.D. dissertation, Bowling Green State University, 1970. Some has also appeared in the following sources, for which I gratefully acknowledge the cooperation of editors and publishers as indicated:

"A Brief Observation Concerning Jesse Stuart's Man in Nature" reprinted from *Pegasus* (Special Memorial Issue 1975). Copyright © 1975 *Pegasus,* Kentucky State Poetry Society, Route 1, Old Boston Road, Lebanon Junction, Kentucky 40150.

"A Concept of the Image in the Poetry of Jesse Stuart" reprinted from *South* 4 (Summer 1972). Copyright © 1972 *South,* Department of English, Stetson University, DeLand, Florida 32720.

"A Record of the Dream: The Image in Practice" reprinted from *Jesse Stuart: Selected Criticism,* edited by J. R. LeMaster. Copyright © 1978 J. R. LeMaster. Reprinted by permission of the publishers, Valkyrie Press, Inc., 2135 First Avenue South, St. Petersburg, Florida 33712.

"Jesse Stuart: Sonneteer" reprinted from *Jack London Newsletter* 10 (May-August 1977). Copyright © 1977 *Jack London Newsletter,* Department of Foreign Languages and Literatures, Southern Illinois University, Carbondale, Illinois 62901.

"Jesse Stuart: The Man and His Poetry" reprinted from *American Book Collector* 20 (Summer 1970). Copyright © 1970 *American Book Collector,* 1822 School Street, Chicago, Illinois 60618.

"Jesse Stuart's *Album of Destiny:* In Pursuit of Whitman's Parallels" reprinted from *Ball State University Forum* 13 (Winter 1972). Copyright © 1972 Ball State University, Muncie, Indiana 47306.

"Jesse Stuart's *Album of Destiny:* In Whitman's Eternal Flow" reprinted from *Illinois Quarterly* 36 (September 1973). Copyright © 1973 *Illinois Quarterly,* News and Publications Services, Illinois State University, Normal, Illinois 61761.

Contents

Preface

I first heard of Jesse Stuart when I was in the sixth grade. I attended a township school in Southern Ohio at that time, and one day during story-telling hour a young man told a remarkable tale about life in the hills. When the teacher asked where he got his story, he replied, "My Uncle Jesse wrote it." Years later, just after I returned home from a tour of duty in the U.S. Navy, I drove up W-Hollow and knocked on the Stuarts' door. I introduced myself to Naomi Deane, Jesse's wife, and she explained that he was taking a nap. That was nearly a year following the almost fatal heart attack that he suffered in Murray, Kentucky, on October 8, 1954, and he was still recuperating. Mrs. Stuart assured me that Jesse would speak to me if I returned later, and I took her at her word. When I returned that evening Jesse met me at the door. Standing there and staring at a big man, a hulking man, I realized that I had come without anything in particular to say. Sensing that I felt awkward, he invited me in and we talked.

To this day I don't know why I drove up W-Hollow road to meet Jesse Stuart, but I have always been glad that I did. I found a man whom I could admire, and since that time I have discovered a large body of literature which I can also admire. My discovery of the literature began when I read *The Thread That Runs So True,* as an undergraduate, and has continued through book after book. During the latter part of the Sixties I did a Ph.D. dissertation on Jesse's poetry, and this study began there. Since that time I have published ten or a dozen papers on his poetry. I have reviewed his books. I have edited collections of essays concerning him and his writing. And I have always been in touch through correspondence, keeping myself informed about his career. Realizing that his poetry and mine have little in common, I continue to admire the man and his work. I continue to believe that heretofore he has been too little read and too little appreciated.

This study, then, is the result of my having read Jesse's poetry over the last twenty years, and of having written about it for the last ten. It has come a long way from the dissertation that I completed in 1970, and I trust that there is still a long way to go before the final chapter on his career as a poet has been written. In the meantime I remain grateful for the encouragement and counsel given me by Fred Eckman and Alma Payne as I did the dissertation. I am also grateful to those editors who over the years have found my essays about Stuart's poetry worthy of publication. To Frances Weber, who has typed and retyped hundreds of pages of manuscript for me, I owe a great debt. And to my lovely wife, Wanda, I take this opportunity to express my appreciation and love. Without her understanding and perseverance this study would never have begun.

J. R. LeMaster
Baylor University

Jesse Stuart

1

The Making of a Poet:
An Overview

Jesse Stuart has published approximately forty books, and he does not count *Harvest of Youth,* his first volume of verse. With several more in the making, he does not need to. He is, and has been for more than forty-five years, a very prolific writer. A recent bibliography[1] lists single publications for approximately two thousand poems, and several hundreds of short stories. With ten novels, twelve collections of short stories, five volumes of verse, and four biographical books to his credit, he is being read (or has been) in England, Ireland, Denmark, Sweden, Norway, Iceland, Germany, Holland, Switzerland, France, Poland, Czechoslovakia, Russia, Italy, Egypt, Syria, Jordan, Lebanon, Saudi Arabia, Kuwait, West Pakistan, Philippines, Republic of Free China, Japan, Korea, South Africa, Australia, New Zealand, Canada, Brazil, and throughout much of South America.[2]

Stuart has traveled over much of the world as a goodwill ambassador for the Department of State. He has taught and lectured abroad, including a year at the American University, Cairo, Egypt. In 1937 he received a Guggenheim Fellowship in order to go to Scotland and study the origins of the literature, and the culture in general, of his Appalachian region. He

---

1. Hensley C. Woodbridge, *Jesse and Jane Stuart: A Bibliography* (Murray, Kentucky, 1969), pp. 3-89.
2. Sister Mary Carmel Browning, *Kentucky Authors: A History of Kentucky Literature* (Evansville, Indiana, 1968), p. 73.

has been awarded twelve honorary doctor's degrees,[3] some of which are from such institutions as Baylor University and the University of Kentucky. The city of Greenup, Kentucky, has erected a monument in his honor, and Murray State University houses Stuartana in the suite of three rooms set aside especially for that purpose. Valley Station, Kentucky, now has a Jesse Stuart High School, and prior to the death of David Brandenburg, founder of Harvest Press in Cincinnati, there was a magazine for Stuart "buffs" entitled *W-Hollow Harvest* (1967-1968). The list of honors that have been bestowed upon him is long and impressive, and one of them, in which he has considerable pride, is the five-thousand-dollar award given by the Academy of American Poets.

Stuart has been known primarily as a popular writer, and his reputation rests largely upon his prose. He has, nevertheless, produced a significant body of poetry which has received remarkably little critical attention. In spite of the fact that the tendency has been to dismiss him as relatively insignificant, we cannot dismiss him for being a regionalist (assuming that regionalism is bad, out of vogue, or both) any more than we can dismiss Faulkner for the same reason. Nor can we dismiss him for being autobiographical, any more than we can dismiss Thomas Wolfe for the same reason. We cannot dismiss him for being pastoral, any more than we can dismiss Robert Frost. His patriotism, his egotism, his virility, his humor, his preoccupation with death, and his undying optimism can all be found in many of the best writers of our time.

Although Stuart scholarship has been sparse, there are some very encouraging signs that it will not remain so. Wood-

---

3. For these and other awards see Woodbridge, pp. xv-xvii. Also see "Jesse Stuart: Awards and Honors" in Mary Washington Clarke, *Jesse Stuart's Kentucky* (New York, 1968), pp. vii-viii. Stuart recently mailed me a chronology (dated January 31, 1977) compiled by Jack Jernigan, Louisville, Kentucky, which stipulates that there are now fourteen honorary degrees. Also, in addition to the five volumes of poems listed by Woodbridge there are now two volumes of selected poems.

bridge, in the "Preface to the Second Edition" of his bibliography, summarizes the situation:

> The past eight years have seen a growing scholarly interest in the study of Stuart's life and works. This can be measured by the appearance of *W-Hollow Harvest* (1967-1968) edited by David and Phyllis Brandenburg, the doctoral dissertations of Eve Blair and Frank Leavell, an increased number of M.A. theses and the appearance between October 1967 and December 1968 of four book-length studies, those of Eve Blair, Lee Pennington, Mary Washington Clarke, and Ruel Foster.[4]

Of the four books, Pennington's is a study of symbolism in the novels; Blair's, a survey of the poet's life and work; Clarke's, a fascinating study of folklore in his writing; while Foster attempts to treat the novels, short stories, poetry, and give some account of various events in the poet's life. Also, since Woodbridge revised his bibliography two other books have been published: Wade Hall's *The Truth Is Funny: A Study of Jesse Stuart's Humor*, Indiana Council of Teachers of English, 1970, and Dick Perry's *Reflections of Jesse Stuart*, McGraw-Hill, 1971. Perry's book, written from a series of taped interviews, contains much popular appeal, although it is limited in scholarly interest. Hall's book, on the other hand, should prove valuable to future scholars. It examines sources and devices of humor in both the fiction and the poetry.

Ruel E. Foster, in and out of his book on Stuart, has shown great interest in the short stories and in story-telling techniques. In one of his essays he exalts Stuart as a master story-teller:

> Jesse Stuart is a writing man. He is a genuine, original, marvelously fecund writing man, and the unduly fretful twentieth century does not quite know what to do with him, how to classify him, what attitude to take towards

---

4. P. vii. Lee Oly Ramey wrote in a letter dated August 30, 1969, that he is doing research for a book-length study.

him. As a result, it has so far walked around him, shaken its head at him, and refused to talk about him because it could not quite comprehend him.[5]

Foster makes a number of observations about the prose that are equally applicable to the poetry—for example, that the poet contemplates the life about him and then puts his contemplations into words, that he is more interested in living than in writing, and that the bulk of what he has written consists of projecting his eastern Kentucky milieu into a fictional world.

Equally characteristic of his poetry is his famous "talk-style," deriving from the tall tale of the frontier. Like Hemingway, he has borrowed his short sentence from Mark Twain; and in the poetry, sentence and line often correspond. In both poetry and prose, Foster observes, Stuart is good at writing dialect. Like his poetry, his prose is full of visual and auditory images—so much so that Foster says: "What Robert Frost is to the sound-posture of poetry, Jesse Stuart is to the sound-posture of fiction."[6] In effect, he is a poet who writes in prose, partially because he is in a prose world—one that has increasingly had science on the brain. Regardless of the medium, he keeps his reader constantly absorbed in sounds, odors, and images of an outdoor world. "Stuart is," says Foster, "primarily a *maker,* a *poet.* He has a feeling for the life of things. He depicts things exactly and lets the universal shine through."[7]

Seldom has a writer assimilated his milieu so completely, and seldom has one been so completely assimilated by his milieu. Throughout his literary career the poet has made

---

5. "Jesse Stuart, Short Story Writer," *Reality and Myth: Essays in American Literature*, ed. William E. Walker and Robert L. Welker (Nashville, Tennessee, 1964), p. 145.
6. *Ibid.*, p. 157.
7. *Ibid.*, p. 159.

numerous references to himself as "brother to the tree,"[8] and the most vivid image the reader comes away with is that of two human feet (without socks and shoes) buried two or three inches in yellow Kentucky clay. As the lineage in his *Beyond Dark Hills* indicates, he belongs to the "tall figures of earth":

> Now here are the men of earth I am directly descended from—both sides are sturdy mountaineers. On the Stuart side are workers, fighters, heavy drinkers, and men of physical endurance. Among the Hiltons are lovers of flashy colors, book readers and people religiously solid as their hills.
>
> And now the old generations are sleeping upon the high Kentucky hills amid the primitive lands they cleared and close to the log houses they made. . . . That was the day when tall figures of the earth were needed.[9]

John Bird, onetime editor of *Saturday Evening Post* and lifelong friend of Stuart's, says that the W-Hollow writer came into the eighteenth century when he was born in 1907, and certainly not into the twentieth.[10] The songs that were sung by his people were handed down by word of mouth. They carried old ballads and tunes, stories, and detailed family histories in their memories. John Bird is not the only one to point out that Stuart is an anachronism. Foster considers his literature to be "a nostalgic evocation of a vanished past."[11] Dayton Kohler, in an article on the poet and James Still, agrees. Everything Stuart writes, contends Kohler, points back to "the

---

8. *Man with a Bull-Tongue Plow* (New York, 1934) p. 126. Such references are scattered throughout Stuart's work. Further references to MWBTP included in the text.

9. *Beyond Dark Hills* (New York, 1938), p. 25. In this early autobiographical book Stuart tells his own story. Further references to BDH included in the text.

10. "My Friend Jesse Stuart," *Saturday Evening Post* 232 (July 25, 1959), 79.

11. "Jesse Stuart, Short Story Writer," p. 159.

anonymous story-tellers of the frontier."[12] Both writers, he continues, write the "westering American dream" in the language of the people who lived that dream.

Isolation played its part in his early development as a poet. When he was fifteen, he went to Camp Knox (now Fort Knox) for a summer training program, and that was his first time to travel more than fifty miles from home (BDH, p. 52). As late as his enlistment in the U.S. Navy, after attending Lincoln Memorial and Vanderbilt, there was no road up W-Hollow. One had to walk it. He explains in *Beyond Dark Hills* how the family early moved from a one-room shack to a three-room shack, and finally to one with four rooms. When someone moved close enough for the chickens to mix with those of the neighbors, the Stuarts moved on. In *God's Oddling* he writes:

> I myself remember the days when snow lay on the ground from November until March, and we children lived in a small land-locked world with no books, victrolas, or radios to amuse us. We didn't get a paper or a magazine and had to depend on our imaginations and what nature provided for our entertainment.[13]

Within the isolated world of W-Hollow, the first and perhaps greatest influence on Jesse's becoming a poet was his father. In this biography of his father he tells of his father's intense love for the land, and of how his father brought poetry out of the earth. His father, he says, was an uneducated "poet of the earth":

> My father didn't have to travel over the country searching for something beautiful to see. He didn't have to go away to find beauty, for he found it everywhere around

---

12. "Jesse Stuart and James Still, Mountain Regionalists," *College English* 3 (1942), 525.

13. *God's Oddling* (New York, 1960), p. 33. Further references to GO included in the text.

him. . . . He found so many strange and beautiful things that I tried to rival him by making discoveries, too. I looked into the out-of-way and unexpected places to find the beautiful and the unusual. (pp. 38-39)

This early and serious looking into things led to a philosophy in which nature plays a trick on man. "The seasons came over and over again in the hills," he observed, "but people last only a short time" (BDH, p. 35). Elsewhere he tells how his sister Sophia, at the age of seven, explained death to him and illustrated by smashing a big black ant between two rocks.[14] In *God's Oddling* he says of those early days of intense observation, "But even among these hills eternal in their great beauty of lilting green leaves in the wind—no one could stop time" (pp. 80-81). Because "no one could stop time" one finds throughout his writing an Ecclesiastical lament for the brevity of life.

The second personal influence on Jesse's becoming a poet was his mother. She came from the "bookish Hiltons," and she early encouraged her son to read, dream, and—most of all—to dream of an education. The boy considered his mother very artistic. When his father was ill, his mother wove baskets from wood and young Jesse peddled them around the countryside to keep the family going (BDH, p. 39). He also tells of how she would go into the fields and the woods looking for a wild flower that she particularly liked. When she found it, she sat for hours making the same kind of flower with quilt pieces (BDH, p. 52).

The third person to influence Jesse significantly never lived in W-Hollow and was far removed from him in time. When the poet was a sophomore in high school, and walking through the hills to and from school, his English teacher, Mrs. Robert Hattan, introduced him to the poetry of Robert Burns. In Burns he found a literary hero, a farmer-poet with whom he could identify. Stuart's ancestors on his father's side came

---

14. *The Year of My Rebirth* (New York, 1956), p. 198. Further references to YR included in the text.

from Scotland. Six tall brothers came from the Firth of Forth and first settled in Virginia, later moving into Kentucky. The young student idolized Burns: "I feasted on the poetry of Robert Burns. . . . And my prayer, if ever I prayed one then, was to write poetry that would endure like the poetry of Robert Burns" (BDH, p. 58). This was also the time he began to write. He took his old dog into the hills at night, and while the dog chased foxes into the early hours of the morning, he lay on the ground and wrote verse by lantern light.

The obsession with Burns cannot be overemphasized. In *Beyond Dark Hills* he tells of how he met Maria Sheen, daughter of a Sandy River farmer. He vowed he would marry her when he met her at Plum Grove Schoolhouse, and his reading of Robert Burns made him even more determined:

> I read where Robert Burns and Highland Mary dipped their hands under the water together, and held Bibles in their other hands. This was a token of eternal engagement. Maria Sheen and I must go to Sandy and do the same thing under the shade of the birch trees. (p. 104)

Kentucky, as he explains, was his land of Robert Burns. The Little Sandy River was the River Ayr. Maria was his Highland Mary, whom he imagined to be tall, strong, slender, and beautiful.

One would likely be tempted to dismiss such fantasy as peculiarly childish were it not for the tribute to Burns in *The Year of My Rebirth*.[15] There Stuart tells again how the Scottish poet changed his life. He tells how, years after his discovery, he went to Scotland, tracing Burns' movements wherever he could. Near Dumfries, at the grave of his hero, he paused to meditate, and to recall the inspiration that had been given to him. As a gesture of humility and profound gratitude, he placed a sprig of Kentucky goldenrod on the grave.

After high school, the poet rebelled against his isolated existence. He was also disillusioned because he had no money,

---

15. See particularly pp. 156-161.

and could not go to college. He left home and traveled with a carnival. Before he left, though, he burned his books. "Life can be put into a book," he observed, "but life cannot be taken from a book. The man that gets life must get down and put his hands on it. He must hide his face in the wet leaves of the earth" (BDH, p. 109). He blamed his reading of books for making him restless. Also, he was determined that James, his brother, would not be driven from the soil by books. Symbolically, his burning of his books was a romantic gesture, a kind of ritual in which he would come out as the phoenix comes from its own ashes. Once and for all, he thought that he would be released from his poetic demon, that he could say goodbye to poetry forever.

Nothing turned out quite the way the young poet planned it. By day he found the carnival exciting, a place "for lovemaking" (BDH, p. 116), but he could not shake his demon by night. In his tent, which he shared with a clown, he wrote about the hills, about Maria Sheen, and about his dream of going to college. Many nights he simply could not sleep. He would go to bed determined not to get up, but inevitably he would get up and he often wrote all night. "I was not mastering poetry," he writes, "but it was mastering me. I just couldn't help writing poetry" (BDH, p. 117). A few lines from two of his sonnets for Maria illustrate what he was writing, and how it was grounded in his early contemplation of detail which rivaled that of his father:

> The raincrow croaked for a down-pour rain,
> The lizard roved the scaly bark for sun
> While Maria Sheen sat closer by my side.
> I do not know if water kissed the grain
> And if that lizard found his patch of sun,
> But I do know who said she'd be my bride.
>
> (BDH, p. 118)

The second example is especially interesting because it uses the old device of describing one's lady in terms of images from nature. For the poet, the lady is both like and is an integral part of nature:

> Her skin is milk-weed dark, her eyes sky-blue,
> Her teeth are blood-root white, her hair is black
> As thick rain-clouds . . . her lips are soft as new
> Bark peeled from a slippery-elm and her back
> Is straight as a horse weed upon the shore.
>
> (BDH, p. 118)

Ever since his childhood days at Plum Grove School the poet had dreamed of going to Harvard. He knew nothing about Harvard, although he had heard that it was a school with a tradition. Dismissed from the carnival, and feeling deeply his old desire to go to college, he turned to exploring possible alternatives. His thoughts, he says, were about the sea. Broke and feeling dejected, he composed these lines:

> Harvard or the Sea
> I have lived my youth in one unsettled state
> And months of barren earth is life too much for me.
> The glorious close will bring me Harvard or the sea.
> Nine months earth-prisoned! How can I bear to wait?
> Since I was twelve, I have been foot-free to the soil;
> Pocketless a dime, I've rambled through many a town
> When the winter moon and silver stars slanted down;
> Bunked with toughs; did them a tremendous toil;
> Met pals, forgot; stopped and took my school life stay.
> Now within Harvard's halls there is one life for me.
> Another life is on waste water's blue immensity
> That will make me turn my back on home, forget the day
> My feet were bound to earth. Then Great Seducer Sea,
> Be last to pant and lick your wet lips over me.[16]

The lines contain unimpressive poetry, but Stuart was not yet eighteen. Although the poem is little more than prose state-

---

16. BDH, p. 120. These and some of the lines on the following pages actually appeared in *Harvest of Youth* (1930) before the publication of *Beyond Dark Hills* (1938). The first draft of *Beyond Dark Hills* was written in 1932.

ment, it could have had much value to the young poet as a means of talking his way through a crisis. In the last two lines, the sea as a seducer panting and licking wet lips appears to be a successful image. Even though they fail as poetry, the lines do record the youth's sense of dejection.

After the carnival job, Stuart went to Camp Knox. While he was there, he went to Louisville and bought everything he could find on Edgar Allan Poe. He also bought a volume of Burns and stole *Carlyle's Essay on Burns* from the post library because no one would sell it to him.[17] When he left Camp Knox and took a job with Armco Steel in Ashland, he was reading enthusiastically. The change was good. For the first time in his life he could afford to buy books.

The work at the mill was exhausting, but it did not exhaust his demon. Every week he bought a new book of poetry and read it in his room at night. He read Rupert Brooke, Alan Seeger, Amy Lowell, Robert Frost, Sara Teasdale, Edna Millay, and Edwin Markham. This was his first encounter, he writes, with the new poetry, the poetry of his contemporaries and near-contemporaries. He does not say whether he was reading such poets as Yeats, Eliot, and Pound. He read Sandburg, though, with mixed feelings. He loved Sandburg's poetry about the soil, but was convinced that Sandburg had no business writing about steel. In a bitter diatribe, he facetiously refers to Sandburg as "the singer of steel," and lashes out at the man who was later to become a close friend:

> I am reading your books because I work in steel now. I know you have never worked in steel.
>
> If you have worked there, you had a snap. Carl Sandburg, you don't know anything about steel. You got your ideas from walking around the mills at night or talking to the Mayor of Gary, Indiana. Go on and write

17. The title here is as it appears in BDH, p. 128. The reference, however, may be to the essay in Thomas Carlyle, *Critical and Miscellaneous Essays* (Boston, 1869), I, 256-314. This was reprinted from *Edinburgh Review* No. 96.

your excellent poems about the wheat fields and the sun-
flowers in the wind and the great open spaces of the sun-
down west, but Carl Sandburg, lay off writing about
steel. Don't disillusion people about the beauty of steel
and about the steel birdman that drones and drones in
the blue, blue sky. And whatever you do, quit singing
about the beauty of steel. (BDH, pp. 141-142)

One sees here a maxim that Stuart, after his Vanderbilt
days, would state publicly, and would subscribe to in every-
thing he wrote. There would be no objectivity for him, no
aesthetic distance. The writer, he would insist, has to be an
intimate part of what he writes.

While working at the mill, the poet lived in a boarding
house that had a reputation for being tough. He borrowed
money from "Red Hot Mattie," the boarding-house prostitute,
and constantly pampered his demon. What he wrote was
highly autobiographical, coming out of immediate experi-
ence. Working on the night shift, he composed lines about
sleep:

> There are seconds in our lives that pass
> Us down like long dark alley ways of dreams.
> We drift like leaves on currentless streams
> Out beyond all time and whirling mass
> Of space. Softly we sink, . . . (BDH, p. 160)

After losing a fight to a steel-mill tough, he wrote "Batter Me
Down, Life":

> Batter me down, you who are strong, I plead.
> I who am weak, in the little ways I know
> Will learn to battle young and soon take heed.
> Batter me down, as rain beats grasses low!
> (BDH, p. 161)

The poem sounds remarkably like these lines from Carl
Sandburg's "Prayers of Steel":

Lay me on an anvil, O God.
Beat me and hammer me into a crowbar.
Let me pry loose old walls.
Let me lift and loosen old foundations.[18]

In further consideration of influence, one should not overlook that John Donne's "Batter my heart, three-personed God" could have figured greatly in the writing of either poem, or both. Stuart, in all candor, has admited his debt to Sandburg: "My earlier poems will show what Carl Sandburg meant to me. His impressions upon me are definitely shown in my earliest poems, a slender volume, *Harvest of Youth,* published privately in 1930."[19]

He was more than ever excited about the possibility of going to college, and even though it looked as if he would never be there, he wrote "Stanza on Leaving College":

My room lights sink, outside the night winds moan;
The hour approaches I strike the world alone.
Then forget me not for I shall think of you,
And this my last dear friends, adieu! adieu!
                    (BDH, p. 152)

At least once, while he was at the boarding house, he became so disillusioned that he burned his poems, but he started all over again. Finally, with thirty dollars in his pocket, he walked out of the steel mill, determined to go to college. "It was farewell to steel. Farewell," he says, "to the Cool Memories of Steel forever" (BDH, p. 170).

The poet started hitchhiking across Kentucky in search of a college and finally arrived at Lincoln Memorial University in Tennessee. He lied to the dean because he did not have any money (BDH, p. 177), and experience had taught him that one did not get into college without it. Fortunately, he was admitted. While there he exchanged poems with Don West, a ministerial student, and for the first time in his life he met a

---

18. *Complete Poems* (New York, 1950), p. 109.
19. "Sandburg, My Hero," *Lincoln Herald* 70 (Spring 1968), 41.

writer, Harry Harrison Kroll. Kroll was his teacher, and Stuart writes of him in *Beyond Dark Hills*: "I worshiped the ground he walked on because he was a writer" (p. 218). Kroll encouraged his student to submit to magazines, and the feeling of success that came from submitting resulted in a deluge of approximately five hundred poems before he left Lincoln Memorial (BDH, p. 219).

One is always impressed in reading *Beyond Dark Hills* that it is intentionally the autobiography of a young poet—of a young man who thinks of himself as a poet. Stuart also wrote many stories while he was at Lincoln Memorial, but they do not appear to have meant as much to him. He had differences with Professor Kroll about structuring stories. His teacher wanted him to plot stories, using O. Henry as a model. But in spite of the advice of his teacher he insisted upon following the example of Maupassant, whom he had read in high school. Some of the stories were published later: "Forty-three of the pieces that I wrote while at Lincoln Memorial were later published in *Esquire, North American Review,* and other magazines."[20] As editor of *The Blue and the Gray,* the student newspaper at Lincoln Memorial, he published some of his own poems as early as 1927. By the end of his senior year, in 1929, his poems had begun to appear in such "little" magazines as *American Poet, Sonnet Sequences, Kentucky Folklore,* and *Poetry.* A year later his articles began to appear. "The Value of Well Kept Yards," which was a theme written in high school, was published in *Home Circle* in April of 1930.

Lincoln Memorial was an important landmark in Stuart's development as a poet. In the first place, he finally admitted to himself that he belonged to the hills, and that he could never stay away from them very long. "There is something good about the old country life that is passing," he writes. "It is the real sweetness of living down against the soil. And that life will never come again" (BDH, p. 200). Secondly,

---

20. Interview taped at W-Hollow, May 31, 1971.

he finally accepted his demon: "The urge was part of me. It would not leave. I wanted to put things into words. Words were living things. Verse was living words combined to make a living body and a living force that would be felt" (BDH, p. 219). And third, he declared his literary independence. His verse, from high school until he left Lincoln Memorial, was full of obvious influences by Carl Sandburg, Robert Frost, A. E. Housman, Edna St. Vincent Millay, and even John Donne. Upon leaving, he wrote: "I didn't want to write like Robert Burns now. I wanted to write like myself. I wanted to be myself. . . . I wanted to be different, not for the sake of being different but being different for something" (BDH, p. 229).

It is difficult to know what to make of such a declaration. In the first place, tracing influences is often as futile and misleading in Stuart's work as in that of any other poet. In the second place, a writer can be held responsible for conscious influences; all others remain mysterious and inexplicable. Although he has been saying for most of his writing career that he has never attempted to imitate anyone, the influences are obvious enough to prompt statements like this: "All the great English naifs are suggested for comparison at one time or another—name them at random: Blake, Burns, Clare, even Cowper, Goldsmith, the young Wordsworth."[21] Orrick Johns is referring to *Man with a Bull-Tongue Plow,* though he could have written the same thing about any of the poet's collections.

Anyone who attempts to explain influences upon the poems should bear in mind two or three important developments. First, Stuart early worked out techniques of pictorial representation which have remained. Second, he has given much thought to how memory functions, or at least to

---

21. Orrick Johns, "Book-of-the-Month Club News," ed. Harry Scherman. Along with thousands of other items of incomplete data, this is contained in Stuart's scrapbooks, which are housed in the library at Murray State University, Murray, Kentucky. This item appears in Scrapbook 1934-1935, p. 9.

how his functions. In essays entitled "Memory Practices"[22] and "Memory Albums,"[23] he writes about the memory as though it were a camera. Memories become images and are stored for future retrieval. In "Memory Albums," memorizing rose bushes is compared to memorizing poems. The poet memorizes the landscape of a poem, the physical details; he photographs it. Third, given the idea of a photographic memory, and T. S. Eliot's idea that all of the tradition shapes itself in each emerging poem—or that an emerging poem becomes the archetype for all poems—one can more readily perceive the meaning of "influence" as it applies to the poet's writing practices. "Influence" simply does not equal "imitation." Orrick Johns is quite accurate in his observations, but he falls short of contributing anything toward a better or more perceptive reading of the poems, and all because he makes no distinctions between conscious imitation and other-than-conscious influence. Apparently, the images that are stored in the memory are not all tagged sufficiently to indicate whether they originally came from a poem, or from life. Even if they were, it might not make a difference: "For standing in a leaf storm is the greatest poetry on earth."[24]

During the year following graduation from Lincoln Memorial, Stuart was principal of Warnock High School, in eastern Kentucky. But in 1931, he left his hills once again. As a poet, he was still unknown. He went to Vanderbilt, attracted by such names as Donald Davidson, Donald Wade, Walter Clyde Curry, Robert Penn Warren, and John Crowe Ransom. When he arrived, he met Don West again, but refused West's advice to enroll in the School of Religion (BDH, p. 282). He stayed, although he had no money to buy books. He was too proud to borrow or to ask for help. Consequently, his exams made poor impressions on his teachers. He was in extreme poverty, living on eleven meals a week. Before each class, he filled his stomach with water to escape being embarrassed by

22. *Kappa Delta Pi Record* 8 (April 1972), 112-113.
23. *Tennessee Teacher* 37 (February 1970), 9.
24. "Memory Practices," p. 113.

its growling, which caused the girls around him to laugh.[25] But even while he was hungry, his poetic demon drove him. "It was just in me to write poetry," he says, "and I did not suppress the desire. Poetry took me along. It made me its servant. I couldn't handle poetry. . . . Poetry will tell you to let the term papers go to hell. It will make you lie to your teachers" (BDH, pp. 284-285). Feeling his dejection deeply once again, he wrote:

> The leafless tree in winter stands alone
> Dreaming of leafy days and sunny Spring
> When birds alighted in her boughs to sing.
> Now somewhere out by changing winds I'm blown,
> A yellow leaf to drift with time away
> The silver moments of my swift brief day.
>   (BDH, p. 290)

The Fugitives, for the most part, were either teaching or had gone elsewhere. The word "agrarianism" was in the air, but the closest thing the poet could find to represent agrarianism around Vanderbilt was a few tomato plants in Donald Davidson's back yard.[26] Davidson, be that as it may, took an interest in him, as did Robert Penn Warren and Edwin Mims. He also visited Sidney Hirsch, a Jewish intellectual and world traveler who had actively encouraged the Fugitives by making his home available as a meeting place. "Robert Frost had been there," he writes, "and G. K. Chesterton, Clarence Darrow, Edwin Markham, George Russell, Vachel Lindsay, and T. S. Eliot" (BDH, p. 323). He slipped his poems under Donald Davidson's door, and Davidson read them closely, making

---

25. Frank Hartwell Leavell, "The Literary Career of Jesse Stuart" (Unpublished Ph.D. dissertation, Vanderbilt University, 1965), p. 58. Leavell tells of Stuart's battle with the stomach, but he adds (p. 67) that Donald Davidson, in an interview, personally told him of Stuart's poverty. Stuart's own account of the battle is found in BDH, pp. 311-313.

26. *Ibid.*, p. 62. On May 12, 1970, Stuart told me that Leavell is wrong. The plants, he said, were in Robert Penn Warren's back yard.

suggestions about revising. Davidson encouraged him to submit to reputable journals and to return to his W-Hollow milieu where he could write about what he knew and loved.

In order to stay in school the last quarter, he forged Don West's name to a promissory note (BDH, p. 316). Later, he told his friend about it. Wesley Hall, where Stuart lived, burned on February 19, 1932, two years after *Harvest of Youth* was published. And although a trunk filled with manuscripts burned, along with his clothes and his unfinished Master's thesis, it did not mean that he had lost all of his poems. He went home without a degree, but in the meantime had become a poet. Before the summer ended he would have poetry accepted by *American Mercury, Poetry,* and *Virginia Quarterly Review.* These publications would lead to a contract from E. P. Dutton and Company for *Man with a Bull-Tongue Plow,* a mammoth collection of 703 sonnets and "near-sonnets."

Once he was home from Vanderbilt, he walked the hills for several days and made a new pact with nature. He bared his back to the sun, and again he followed the plow. At the end of the field, he stopped his mules for rest; and while they were resting he wrote. He wrote on almost everything, and he wrote almost everywhere. He wrote on used envelopes, on paper bags, on tobacco pouches, and on poplar leaves. He used a twig to inscribe his poem on a leaf, and in the evening he took the leaf home where he could follow the impressions and copy the poem onto a piece of paper (BDH, pp. 338-339). In eleven months he had turned out at least sixty per cent of the 703 poems in *Man with a Bull-Tongue Plow.*

Before going to Vanderbilt, Stuart had had his juvenilia, *Harvest of Youth,* printed privately. After Vanderbilt, he became ashamed of his slender volume of experimental verse. He did not realize that the book had genuine value, that it revealed the range of his experiments, and that it recorded something of the range of intense reading which began in the steel mill. In the poem "Silhouettes," for example, he tried to write like an Imagist:

> Hard, clean
> Chiseled profiles
> Of black bodied trees
> Swerving in the wind
> At sundown.[27]

In a number of poems he attempted a Sandburgian kind of free verse. One sees vestiges of Sandburgian verse, in spite of an awkward attempt to break the poem into paragraphs, in "Steel Gang":

> Listen: we were dogging steel, somewhere,
> Between Six Hickories and Maldraugh Hill . . .
> Daring, stormy . . . we chewed tobacco and flapped
> Broad-rimmed and dusky felt hats . . . (p. 38)

One can see Frost in "The Wind Has Ways," and John Donne in "Batter Me Down, Life." Also, Lee Oly Ramey has pointed out that Rupert Brooke influenced the young poet, illustrating his contentions with Brooke's "The Great Lover" and Stuart's "Things I Have Loved."[28]

Influences are both obvious and numerous. One can see them in the prose, too. In *God's Oddling,* for instance, he has his father say to his Uncle Fonse: "It's good fences that we got between our places that make us good neighbors" (p. 73). In describing a mountain funeral, he borrows some of T.S. Eliot's images of desolation: "The crows will fly over here. The wind will blow. The rats will make footprints on the logs and the wind and the rain will change the rat prints. They will smooth them over and the rats will make them again. And thus it

---

27. (Howe, Oklahoma, 1930), p. 32. HY was reprinted by the Council of Southern Mountains in 1964. It was apparently at that time that Hargis Westerfield's Foreword was added. The Foreword was reprinted by permission from "*Harvest of Youth:* Jesse Stuart's First Published Book," *American Book Collector* 13 (February 1963), 23-24. Further references to HY included in the text.

28. See Lee Oly Ramey, "An Inquiry into the Life of Jesse Stuart as Related to His Literary Development and a Critical Study of His Works" (Unpublished M.A. thesis, Ohio University, 1941), pp. 117-118.

happens in the waste land" (BDH, p. 252).

As an early experiment in verse, *Harvest of Youth* is convincing. Somewhere in it Stuart tries most of the devices and techniques known to modern poetry. The third section, "Sonnets: Juvenilia," contains an impressive attempt to make the sonnet a viable form. The poet constructs the lines in his experimental sonnets with from eight syllables to twelve. Occasionally, he uses varying line lengths within the same poem. He changes the meter, arranges lines into different units, and tries a number of rhyme schemes. He attempts about every imaginable innovation in his experimental sonnets.

Periodically, critics have questioned why Stuart would stubbornly persist in perpetuating a form so out of vogue, including the Imagist poet John Gould Fletcher.[29] Sheer stubbornness is likely one answer, for he was once told by a teacher that he could not write sonnets.[30] Other answers relate directly to the nature of his art. He early found the form increasingly attractive for short "flights" of song. He also found that he could group sonnets into sequences, letting each one relate an incident, and thereby develop a narrative. He says about his efforts to use the sonnet: "I had no influence on expanding the sonnet to 16 lines. It was more convenient. I also had another idea about the sonnet which I didn't use, but may use later—ten lines in what is called the octave and eight in the sextet. Make it the octet. This makes the sonnet a better form, less cramped, more flexible."[31] There is certainly precedent enough for poets trying to make the sonnet form viable. A list would have to include such names as Edmund Spenser, William Shakespeare, George Meredith, Gerard Manley

29. "Kentucky Georgics," *Poetry: A Magazine of Verse* 45 (1935), 219.

30. Ramey, p. 106. Stuart also tells of the incident in "Sandburg, My Hero," p. 43.

31. Letter to the writer, July 26, 1969. It was after *Harvest of Youth* that he varied the lines in any one sonnet from thirteen to seventeen.

Hopkins, E. E. Cummings, W. H. Auden, and Merrill Moore.

One cannot accuse Stuart, in Frostian terms, of playing tennis with the net down. By the time of *Man with a Bull-Tongue Plow* (1934), he had done his homework, and he had done it well. During the summer following his return from Vanderbilt, he stopped his plow one day and said to his brother James:

> I'm going to write poetry to suit myself from now on. I'm in a different University. I don't have teachers to tell me this is good or that is good. From now on I'm going to be myself and write to suit myself and the way I damn well please. I've failed all my life and I can't do any worse than I have done. (BDH, p. 338)

The way he "damn well" pleased, of course, led to *Man with a Bull-Tongue Plow* (1934), followed by *Album of Destiny* (1944), *Kentucky Is My Land* (1952), and *Hold April* (1962).

Anyone who attempts to assess Stuart's achievement as a poet will have to look closely at *Man with a Bull-Tongue Plow*. Many of the questions that are frequently asked about his craft are answered there—and some of them in the first two or three poems of the collection. In the first sonnet, he presents himself, the subject of his song, the nature of his song, and the source of his song:

> I am a farmer singing at the plow
> And as I take my time to plow along
> A steep Kentucky hill, I sing my song—
> A one-horse farmer singing at the plow!
> I do not sing the songs you love to hear;
> My basket songs are woven from the words
> Of corn and crickets, trees and men and birds.
> I sing the strains I know and love to sing.
> And I can sing my lays like singing corn,
> And flute them like a fluting gray corn-bird;
> And I can pipe them like a hunter's horn—

All of my life these are the songs I've heard.
And these crude strains no critic can call art,
Yours very respectively, Jesse Stuart.[32]

In the second sonnet he expresses his hope for immortality:

There may be some to love his rustic art
And keep his futile tunes in brain and heart
When he is quiet and sleeps beneath the clay
And has no thought of his past yesterday. (p. 3)

In the third sonnet he repeats that people are essential to his list of themes:

I speak of men that live in my lifetime,
And I speak of the men of yesterday.
I do not care to know if this is art—
These common words born in a common heart. (p. 4)

Stuart's early philosophy—based on a cycle of seasons in which Nature renews herself each spring—supplied him with the organizational pattern for *Man with a Bull-Tongue Plow*. He has written much about resurrection and renewal, as might be surmised from such a title as *The Year of My Rebirth*. In that book he writes: "The man who has never planted a seed in the ground would be the first to doubt the story of the resurrection" (p. 84).

During the journey beyond his dark hills, he documented the events of his life, punctuated them, with poems. When he returned, as indicated in *Man with a Bull-Tongue Plow*, he

---

32. P. 3. The sonnets in MWBTP are numbered with two complete poems appearing on each page. There are a few captions, such as "Voice" or "Grass Speaks." In the Plum Grove sonnets, names are captions, but here too the sonnets are usually numbered. Because of the arranging of two on each page, there seems to be no reason for a double reference—to both the number and the page. Double references will be made where necessary to prevent confusion. One should also know something of what to expect of Stuart's punctuation. The dashes here are characteristic, as are the ellipsis marks in the lines previously quoted from "Steel Gang."

continued to document. For forty-five years he has been writing his chronicle of W-Hollow. Each new book that he publishes, whether poetry or prose, is merely a new chapter in the same chronicle, which simply goes on. Once a new chapter is added, it appears as though it has always been there, or at least it appears as though it should have been.

Fairly recently, Jesse Stuart has repeated some old observations about his own craft, and these cannot be ignored. He has said, for example, that it is impossible for him to belong to any clique, school, or literary movement. He has also explained that there is a story behind each of his poems. "My writing," he says, "is a cataloging of present-day events my friends and I have lived."[33] For him, the happy combination resulting in poetry is one of mood and incident. Without either, he contends, he cannot write.

Stuart's Blue Dreamers, the westering pioneers who conquered the wilderness, are buried in Plum Grove Cemetery, and he often walks across the hills to visit them there. Like the seed a man plants in the soil, they have reproduced themselves in every son and daughter, and it is their story which the poet tells. The chronicle continues, and as each recorded incident disappears into the whole, W-Hollow remains what Stuart has often referred to as "the last carbon copy" of a former day when "tall men of the earth" were needed.[34]

---

33. "Autobiographical Reminiscence," *University of Kansas City Review* 27 (October 1960), 59.
34. "America's Last Carbon Copy," *Saturday Review* 40 (December 28, 1957), 5-7. As elsewhere, Stuart discusses here the danger that progress poses to an old way of life.

2

"The Way of All Flesh":
An Ontological View

One who attempts to appreciate Jesse Stuart's poetry finds himself, time after time, returning to *Beyond Dark Hills*. As chronicler he produces art that is inextricably bound up with his life, and *Beyond Dark Hills* is a seedbed, an early outpouring of themes and ideas that are further developed in later volumes of poetry and prose. *Beyond Dark Hills* contains both poetry and prose, and the circumstances surrounding the writing of it are interesting in themselves.

The poet relates something of the circumstances. At Vanderbilt, he contends, he could not write a passing term paper: "When I started to write a term paper I would write a poem" (BDH, p. 314). Dr. Edwin Mims assigned such a paper, and Stuart was determined to write one. It was to be about eighteen pages long, and there were only a few days in which to write it. Concerned over not having been successful before, he set out to impress his teacher. When he had finished, there were 322 closely written pages: "When I handed Dr. Mims my term paper—'Beyond Dark Hills,' I called it—he sucked his pipe harder than I ever saw him suck it before" (BDH, p. 319).

The student was both pleased and worried. He was pleased because he was convinced that he had done something well; he was worried because he knew that he could hardly expect his professor to read it. The teacher, a bit perplexed by the whole matter, read the paper closely, after which he commented: "I have been teaching school for forty years and I have never read anything so crudely written and yet beautiful, tremendous, and powerful as that term paper you have written" (BDH, p. 320). Various scholars, including Lee Oly Ramey, have checked details with Professor Mims concerning the term paper, only to be referred to the story as Stuart tells it: "There is not much more to say than what Stuart says in his *Beyond Dark Hills*. He tells the story rather accurately. That was, of course, the most remarkable term paper I ever got from a student."[1] Donald Davidson, the following summer, went to Bread Loaf School of English at Middlebury, Vermont. He took the paper and showed it to Theodore Morrison of *Atlantic Monthly*. Morrison interested Little-Brown Publishing Company, but Little-Brown never published it. Several years later Stuart requested that his paper be returned. He then sent it to John Macrae at Dutton Publishing Company. It was finally published by Dutton in 1938, approximately six years after it was written.

Beyond Dark Hills, among numerous other things, contains preliminary observations, of a philosophical kind, about nature, God, man, death, and time. Nowhere is there a coherent theory about these things; nor is there such a coherent theory either in *Harvest of Youth* (1930) or in *Man with a Bull-Tongue Plow* (1934). Rather, one must pick up scattered observations in the early autobiography and trace their development through the latter two books to find that there is a coherent theory about the nature of Being in *Album of Destiny* (1944). Lee Pennington traces the philosophy of Being

---

1. Letter to Ramey, December 2, 1939. Quoted in Lee Oly Ramey, "An Inquiry into the Life of Jesse Stuart as Related to His Literary Development and a Critical Study of His Works" (Unpublished M.A. thesis, Ohio University, 1941), p. 189.

throughout the novels. He refers to it as a "vision of life," and says that it is to be found in all of Stuart's works after *Harvest of Youth*.[2]

The poet's ontological view does not have its origin in *Harvest of Youth,* although he first began to publish it there. Instead, it has its origin in a number of childhood experiences and observations. In *Beyond Dark Hills* he asks a question that has always perplexed him: "Does his [a man's] environment make him or does his blood tell?" (p. 26) As early as April, 1918, the blood-environment issue was a pressing one, and he symbolically rejected influences by both environment and blood: "I had broken a path for myself through the snow. I would not step in my father's broken path. I had said that I would not live among the hills forever and die among them and go back to the dust of the hills" (BDH, p. 69).

Stuart was young when the family moved from Cedar Riffles, and the years there seem to have impressed him strangely. The scenes, he explains, made him love loneliness: "There were sounds and sights of beauty but they were things of loneliness" (BDH, p. 30). The loneliness was intense, and the poet could not escape it: " . . . there are pictures of those snowy hills lodged in the album of my brain" (BDH, p. 31). The family moved to a newly-purchased fifty-acre farm, but it too was desolate, a place of loneliness: "There is something to it that leaves an image on the album of the brain and, like the yellow flame of an old lamp, it flickers often but will not go out" (BDH, p. 46). The "image on the album of the brain," the image which produces the loneliness, apparently never goes out. When he visited New York, he found it a lonely place.

---

2. *The Dark Hills of Jesse Stuart* (Cincinnati, 1967), p. 5. In a letter to the writer (August 30, 1969), Ramey expresses doubt about Pennington's conclusions concerning Stuart's "vision." Leavell, on the other hand, has made some observations about Stuart's journal *The Year of My Rebirth* which would make Pennington's study valid. With *The Year of My Rebirth*, Leavell says, the critics for the first time began to see the organic unity in Stuart's work, a thematic unity found in the recovery theme. See Leavell's dissertation, p. 215.

When he traveled in Europe, he found that it, too, was a place of loneliness.

Loneliness in childhood, loneliness and isolation, led to serious contemplation about nature, man, death, time, and God. On one occasion his mother tried to explain the omnipotence and omnipresence of God. She told him that God could ride on clouds and could do everything. His reaction consisted of an intense desire to be God: "If I could only be God! I wanted to be God" (BDH, p. 72). He explains that he caught birds to defy God (BDH, p. 73), and admits that there is no escaping God as reality: "I had come to know my first lesson about God . . . There was no getting away from a man that rode the clouds and saw through a tree" (BDH, p. 74). The hill way was that one was either "right" with God or was not. Stuart writes: "When I got right with God I would go out on the hilltop. I would put my face down against the wet oak leaves on the ground. I would get rid of the wheelbarrow load of sins I had done" (BDH, p. 75). The face in the wet leaves is perhaps a symbolic rejection of the way of his mountain people, which called for looking up and crying out to God.

An early preoccupation with religion is evident in the poet's returning to this subject many times, and his detailed descriptions of spring revival meetings contain some of his best prose. He writes that he saw the hypocrisy of it all when he caught Preacher Baker and a young woman in the grass along W-Hollow Creek (BDH, p. 77). He saw the social value of great spring revivals and baptizing, but he denounced it all as useless: "I am one of them . . . . Though I stand not against it, I can never join my flesh and blood in their worship. . . . I see no use in it all" (BDH, p. 95).

Besides the early traumatic experiences concerning God and religion, there were experiences involving death, particularly those of his brothers. There was also the problem of the devil, the problem of evil. The deaths of his brothers had a profound impact on the boy. He relates vividly the movement of the funeral train across the fields, ending at his grandfather's farm. The Stuarts, at that time, owned no land on which to bury his brothers, and his mother insisted that they be buried on land owned by the family. He writes: "After I had seen my brothers hauled to my grandfather's farm, I was afraid of Death. He was an evil thing to me" (BDH, p. 95). As a thing of evil, death was constantly associated with the devil in the boy's mind. The devil was always described vividly in mountain revival meetings as the father of hellfire and brimstone. He must have had a very impressive idea of what the devil looked like, for he wrote of his grandfather: "I was afraid of him. He was twice as large as my father and had a great long beard . . . . If I had met Grandpa at night I would have thought he was the Devil" (BDH, p. 17).

As the face down against the wet leaves would indicate, the poet found his God in nature. Frank Leavell observes that Stuart never discusses theological issues. On the contrary, says Leavell, his works show him to be "deeply aware of the presence of God revealed in nature about him."[3] Leavell accepts a single quotation from *Beyond Dark Hills*—"When I think of God, I think of the evening sky in Kentucky" (p. 72)—as a significant summary of Stuart's religion. The God-in-nature mystique, however, is only the beginning of a complex scheme of Being in nature. His thinking on the matter at the time is adequately summarized in this sonnet, added to the original manuscript and appearing on the last page of *Beyond Dark Hills:*

> If youth were just an endless flowing river
> Born in the world of springtime not to fade;
> Youth with its season blossoming forever,
> A glorious river young in spring parade!
> If youth's strong mansions of quick devilish dust
> Would not disintegrate into decay
> Only because that Time has said they must,
> And who is Time to blow youth's breath away!
> And who is he to fling snow in the hair

---

3. "The Literary Career of Jesse Stuart" (Unpublished Ph.D. dissertation, Vanderbilt University, 1965), p. 18.

And blotch the temples with his downy flakes;
A sneak you cannot fight and fight him fair;
Because, Time in the end will get the breaks.
Oh, Youth, forever we must race with Time
For we must quickly bloom in our short season;
One time to work and play and spin a rhyme,
For Time will crumble us without a reason! (p. 399)

There is one final observation in *Beyond Dark Hills* which should not be overlooked, and that is the young poet's discovery of Walt Whitman. Whitman's "grass of graves" becomes important in Stuart's working out a philosophy of Being. "Wasn't Uncle Rank right," he asks, "when he said the fluffy green hair of April would hide all scars?" (BDH, p. 398) The discovery of Whitman cannot be overestimated, as indicated by the fact that he took a 479-line poem called "Whispering Grass" to Donald Davidson about the same time that he took his 322-page term paper to Dr. Mims (BDH, p. 320).

After *Beyond Dark Hills* one sees Whitman in almost everything Jesse Stuart writes. Most obvious in *Harvest of Youth* is "Lilac Elegy." As he has indicated, though, the poems in *Harvest of Youth* were written in high school and college, and many therefore precede the graduate term paper for Dr. Mims. By the time of *Man with a Bull-Tongue Plow,* he was relying heavily on Whitman, and reviewers have often referred to the two writers as belonging together. Henry Christman writes, for example, that he is one of the "few Whitmans, daring to break down accepted forms and create a new poetry."[4] John Duffy writes: "The weakness of Whitman is here—endless palaver."[5] Everetta Love Blair discusses Randall Stewart's critical opinion that Stuart and Thomas Wolfe "should be considered as writing under the influence of

4. Henry Christman, review in *Knickerbocker Press*, October 4, 1934. Found in Scrapbook #2, p. 13.
5. John Duffy, review in *Commonweal* 40 (1944), 169. Also found in Scrapbook #15, p. 10
6. *Jesse Stuart: His Life and Works* (Columbia, South Carolina, 1967), p. xxi.

Whitman."[6] Other critics and reviewers have found reasons for relating the two, and Edwin Mims, Stuart's teacher, has said: "We think inevitably of Whitman's *Leaves of Grass*."[7]

He was attracted to Whitman for a number of reasons. Whitman was a rebel, and Stuart too was out of the main stream. Whitman's loneliness was in many ways like his, but most of all Whitman, a city poet, had articulated in *Leaves of Grass* what the rural poet found for himself in his life among the hills. The significance of Whitman came slowly to him, but by the time of *Album of Destiny* he had gone beyond a mere examination of Whitman's poetry. He had found a philosophy that was complementary to his own.

Although *Album of Destiny* contains a full and coherent statement about the nature of Being, *Harvest of Youth* and *Man with a Bull-Tongue Plow* are important in tracing the development toward that statement. In *Harvest of Youth*, the childhood God-in-the-sky has become God-in-nature, a free God:

> I found him in the rising sap
> In a March sapling tree;
> I found him in the winter wind,
> Blowing wildly and free. (p. 19)

Considered further, though, *Harvest of Youth* proves to be confusing, because the poet has not made up his mind. "The Winner" is an early quatrain:

> Against his will he ran a race with Death.
> His muscles were taut drawn in every limb.
> His team mates saw him falter . . . lose his breath . . .
> They sought to cheer when Death romped by him.
> (p. 24)

---

7. Edwin Mims, review in Nashville paper. Name of paper and date not given. Found in Scrapbook #2, p. 22. Attempts to relate Stuart's work to Whitman's are numerous, but most amount to general remarks such as that made by Mims and are for the most part limited to reviews. In spite of this, Whitman's influence has been more than a passing acquaintance and deserves to be worked out in detail.

Although the lines are rough and can hardly be considered accomplished poetry, they state something of the dilemma that the youth saw as characterizing life. The attitude of defeat expressed in the race with death also occurs in "Black April":

> Only God
> Could beat Flint Sycamore
> When he played his last trump:
> In the loam he battled for bread.
>
> (p. 33)

As a player in the card game, Flint Sycamore loses. As a farmer of the soil, he loses. His race with death takes on a new perspective; it becomes a contest with God. The bitterness in the poem, a consequence of having to be the loser, is obvious, especially in this allusion to the Last Supper:

> Twelve men,
> Are sitting at a picnic table
> White clothed
> With rarest food.
> Life is a pleasure they say,
> And God is kind. (p. 36)

Flint Sycamore's struggle is intense, even though he is defeated. The ending of "Black April" is also bitter, but it suggests a way out of forever losing in the game of cards. Flint Sycamore has been a daring man, bringing life from the earth. In the end, life comes from Flint Sycamore: "April life from the bosom / Of Flint Sycamore" (p. 37).

The futility of "Black April" occurs in many of the poems in *Harvest of Youth*. Pennington has observed, "Nearly every poem in *Harvest of Youth* is concerned with 'death' in some degree."[8] Many of the poems end in death and defeat; others find a way to surpass them. "To Muddy Waters" symbolically conquers death, or at least defies it: "Like some deep singer in the voiceless you fling / Futility to wind and march and sing

---

8. *The Dark Hills of Jesse Stuart*, p. 5.

and sing" (p. 54). "Initial-Scarred Trees" is a poem about the possibility of immortality. It dwells on the transience of man's life, but it also asks:

> "What about the past,
> The dreams and ashes of the past—
> What about it anyway?" (p. 38)

"My City" is also about transience, but it affirms that something remains:

> We came back to be
> A father's father's father
> And a mother's mother's mother
> To blood unborn. (p. 44)

Other poems in the collection concern themselves with what comes out of death. In "Louise," the "youthful bloom / Is crushed to dust." But the poet continues: "Earth prides you with her elements of wind and rain" (p. 56). In "Mountain Funeral" the dead man is immortalized in his blooming apple trees, in his ax, in his plow, and in his field of clover (p. 22).

Still other poems symbolically develop the theme of immortality. In "Undulated Season" the "turbulent young blood" of the woman becomes "March tree sap" (p. 28). This symbolic identification is carried further in "She Ventured Far from God," which is a poem about a girl "once steeped in muted corridors of sin" (p. 80). Her sins are those of hot blood, and she is like "a drooping willow stung by winter rain." When spring comes, like the willow she is revived. Her spring revival contradicts conventional attitudes among hill people about sin. The young woman is revived by nature, not by God. In "Margaret," Jesse Stuart's symbolic woman saunters off into "Spring's snowy rows of apple trees" (p. 52). "Knowing that beauty is all that really pays," Margaret belongs to the natural world, where there is no problem of sin. For the poet, who is less fortunate, sin remains, and is posed in the form of an alternative in "Scars":

> With Life's pitcher broken at the fountain
> Spilling sweet wine of youth to Mother Earth,

> Will we forget that sin . . . or remember
> The demon walking by our side from birth?
>   (p. 80)

"Fugative" indicates which of the alternatives the poet will eventually accept:

> He sleeps a fugative . . . and let him be . . .
> He sleeps . . . he bothers not his own proud kin . . .
> He lies beneath his black-jack saplin tree
> Where knotty roots and moles are prying in.
>   (p. 78)

In as far as it goes, *Harvest of Youth* is an important phase of probing and thinking which is expanded in *Man with a Bull-Tongue Plow*. In the first collection man and God recognizably become parts of the natural world. "With Life's pitcher broken at the fountain," the water, "Sweet wine of youth," comes out of the ground and flows back into the ground. It is with this concept of man as belonging to the natural cycle that Stuart continues to pursue his theory of Being in *Man with a Bull-Tongue Plow*.

Because *Man with a Bull-Tongue Plow* was written hurriedly, it purports to do little more than record. The overall plan was to capture moods in the four seasons of the year. There seems, furthermore, no particular reason for placing any one poem where it now appears. The moods simply came, and were written down quickly and freely, with little attention to matters of form. This "spontaneous overflow," a contrast to conscious artistry, may have been helpful in developing the theory of Being. The theory, at least initially, also had to be unforced and natural. It had to come as subconscious process, and certainly not as some form of intellectual decision. As subconscious process, the working out of the theory would be primarily a matter of poetry and secondarily a matter of philosophy.

On Easter Sunday, in 1931, the poet visited Plum Grove Cemetery. He had in mind a series of poems about the dead.

His idea was to put himself in the place of the dead and record their observations. This brought sharp criticism from reviewers and critics, for it was remarkably like what Edgar Lee Masters had done in his *Spoon River Anthology.* Stuart denies any conscious influence:

> If he [Masters] influenced me, as reviews of *Man with a Bull-Tongue Plow* pointed out, the influence would have to have been subconscious. I must have read parts or all of *Spoon River Anthology* and other poems by Masters. I know I certainly didn't lean toward him. He had written a very mean book about Abraham Lincoln—only Allen Tate had praised then. I knew Masters wasn't for me. So I do not remember any influence.[9]

Whether Masters was a formidable influence makes little difference now. What is important is that the dead people would speak through the poet about life, death, and the nature of Being.

Once the poet had decided that the dead could speak, and that they would be listened to, he also realized that verisimilitude would require that they be spoken about. This allowed him one of the most useful devices in the Plum Grove section, and was a big step in the growth of his theory. He decided that he would use the grass, Whitman's "whispering grass," and that he would let the wind and the seasons have voices of their own.

Furthermore, that he visited the cemetery on Easter Sunday is symbolically significant. The importance of a resurrection "of sorts" was in his mind, and would become an integral part of his theory of Being. Easter Sunday is important to the Christian world, but the Sunday on which the poet visited the cemetery was in April. The symbolic significance of the month of April should be clear enough. One finds it in the first few lines of Chaucer's Prologue to the *Canterbury Tales.* For T. S. Eliot it is the "cruellest month," and for Stuart it is the month of "resurrected spring." The resurrection is not necessarily a Christian one, a supernatural one. On the con-

9. Letter to the writer, August 25, 1969.

trary, it is a natural one, and is readily observable through the grass.

In the two sections of *Man with a Bull-Tongue Plow* which precede the Plum Grove poems, scattered lines are concerned with death, time, and decay as belonging to nature. There are the usual observations about the dead: "How silent the countless billions who have died. / They cannot speak to tell us where they lie" (p. 124). There are the usual expressions of fear: "I am afraid the curtain will be drawn / And leave me to return to grass and stone" (p. 37). Death symbolically becomes night, and life is presented as a journey. Man is one journeying into the night along a "dirty-ribbon road" which is covered by fallen leaves and brush and grass (p. 127). Mountain men who cannot read and write already know something of darkness. In that respect they are "children of the night" (p. 201), but their being illiterate does not lessen their love for life: "And there beside the singing Sandy River / I cried: 'Life, why can't you go on forever!' " (p. 196) There are also questions and expressions about possibilities in death: "If there is new life in the womb of night, / I am ready for to meet you, Death, and fight" (p. 193).

Time, too, becomes important in poems scattered throughout *Man with a Bull-Tongue Plow*. There is a preoccupation with the past that sounds remarkably like Whitman. In "Song of Myself" Whitman writes: "The past is the push of you, me, all, precisely the same, / And what is yet untried and afterword is for you, me, all precisely the same."[10] Stuart writes: "The past is past." But in the same poem he says: "Your age is not—but we're established facts" (p. 137). The facts, the objects, exist in time, but time apparently exists outside the facts. The facts or objects exist in space, but the poet adds: "The past goes somewhere—never coming back, / Part of the past is sleeping on the hill" (p. 98).

Contemplation about the uncertainty of facts leads to a further cry of futility:

10. *Complete Poetry and Prose* (New York, 1948), I, 105. This is the Deathbed Edition and contains Malcolm Cowley's famous Introduction.

Facts are most uncertain, for even stone
Disintegrates into positive decay
And a breath of wind could blow the dust away.
There is futility in everything.
And the thing most beautiful soonest goes—
Beauty of flesh, white fragrance of the rose,
The colored feathers on a rooster's wing.
And when we turn to look upon the past
We find few chosen words are things that last.

(p. 124)

One of the necessary realities found in such passages is that of positive decay. All facts decay, but such is not an end in and of itself. When Kate Dills and her lover were shot, "Their mingled blood ran there under the moon / And sank to roots of grass among their hills" (p. 93). The blood of a dog, in much the same way, runs "in a stream on dead leaves down the hill" (p. 153). It flows back into the earth where grass and flowers grow.

The possibility of oneness with nature is found in various places throughout the collection. The poet says:

Nature improved upon has been destroyed.
Let us go naked, wild, like beasts again!
Let us go nameless strangers to the void. (p. 155)

Such lines sound Whitmanesque: "I think I could turn and live with animals, they are so placid and self contain'd, / I stand and look at them long and long."[11] Although the two views seem to concur, they do so only in part. Whitman's placidity does not exist in Stuart's lines. Whitman accepts animals as animals, but for Stuart they are beasts. The tension is there, as though the poet were suggesting an alternative that is not wholly acceptable. But whether he accepts or not, he recognizes that it is possible for life, in nature, to come out of decay. He knows, he says, "a place where the wild pansies grow /Among dry chips of cow dung" (p. 111). Moreover,

---

11. *Ibid.*, p. 88.

the persona in sonnet number 289 expresses a oneness with nature which is almost convincing:

> I shall feel wet oak leaves close to my skin
> And I shall smell these dead leaves after rains.
> The winter of this life is setting in—
> I do love oak-leaves' coffee-colored stains.
> My body will be stained from head to toes
> And I shall have the oak roots through my skull,
> And fern roots through my lips and eyes and nose.
> Each summer I shall wear loose green in full.
> I think I shall be able to discern
> You and the rain through hard eyes of the trees,
> And I shall hold with fingers of the fern
> The nourishment there is in my dead leaves.
> And I shall taste the oak leaves and the rain.
> I shall not feel the oak roots groove my brain. (p. 149)

The lines are about as naturalistic as one could expect, but whether they are convincing or not depends on whether the final line is a denial of consciousness. Either way, the poet has come close, perhaps succeeded, in placing man in nature in such a way that he loses identity as he is fed upon by oak trees and ferns. Significant to the theory of Being is the question of whether he is ultimately used up, that is, consumed and destroyed by the oaks and ferns, or whether, as indestructible force, he is either transformed or transferred into oaks and ferns.[12]

Interestingly enough, the naturalism is reminiscent of that in the poems of Thomas Hardy. Everetta Love Blair, in her survey, mentions Hardy five times, although she never becomes specific about influences. Preferring to generalize, she makes such statements as this: "As Thomas Hardy spoke for the inarticulate people of his Wessex country, so Jesse Stuart has been the spokesman for his people of the Kentucky hills."[13] Stuart, who is more informative about the possibility,

12. For an interesting comparison see Whitman's "The Compost," *ibid.*, p. 330.
13. *Jesse Stuart: His Life and Works*, p. 4.

makes it clear that he had an intense interest in Hardy shortly before writing *Man with a Bull-Tongue Plow.* Although he did not read Hardy in high school, except for one novel, or at Lincoln Memorial, while at Vanderbilt he read most of the novels and all of the collected poems.[14] It is unlikely that he thought of himself as another Thomas Hardy, but that his collection followed so closely after his concentrated reading may mean that the impetus for his naturalistic poems is to be found in Hardy.

The voices of the dead in the Plum Grove section primarily tell stories about life, very much in the way that Masters' dead people do in *Spoon River Anthology.* The poet, in the meantime, becomes increasingly significant as a voice. In the first two sections, he remains relatively outside the poetry and lets his characters speak freely. In the Plum Grove poems, by contrast, he conducts a running dialogue with his Whispering Grass. In the final section, entitled "Preface for After Death," the poet presumes himself dead. He speaks as Jesse Stuart the poet, from the grave. This final section is directed or addressed to Donald Davidson, his teacher at Vanderbilt, and consists primarily of poems of farewell along with a number of poems recording events from the poet's life and work. He takes his place among the Blue Dreamers at Plum Grove Cemetery, and as far as his theory of Being is concerned, a few lines from the last two poems adequately summarize. For his teacher, Stuart figuratively summarizes his own life on earth:

> A white oak leaf the early frost has curled
> Is my experience, Donald Davidson,
> When I think of myself in the past world.
> (p. 361)

The last poem in *Man with a Bull-Tongue Plow* begins with death and decay:

> "Lie still," the fern has said, "there is a reason."
> Muscles are lifeless in a body dead—

---

14. Letter to the writer, June 14, 1972.

A body dead and corn sprung from its bosom. (p. 361)

In the poem the body is claimed by oak limbs, clover, briars, and warm clay. Again the naturalistic process is at work. The poem ends with an expression of doubt about the possibility of a Christian resurrection: "Now if there is a Resurrection Day / I shall be one that's taken by surprise" (p. 361).

As indicated earlier, one of the poet's accomplishments toward developing his ontological view lies in his introducing the Whispering Grass into the Plum Grove poems. The grass is both impersonal and universal. As Whitman says in "Song of Myself": "This is the grass that grows wherever the land is and the water is, / This is the common air that bathes the globe."[15] The grass has a voice, but it also functions in other ways. For example, dead people speak: "The strength of us is in each sweet grass stem; / The strength of us is in each leaf and flower" (p. 264). *Man with a Bull-Tongue Plow* reflects Whitman's idea of efflux only in a limited way. The grass may "transpire from the breasts of young men,"[16] but the poet seems to stop there. He says nothing about influx, and he has far to go before he can say with Whitman that nothing collapses. Rather, he holds to his childhood observation: "People last only a short time. Nature plays a trick on them. She stays young forever" (BDH, p. 35). At the end of the collection, people remain "No more than dog tracks in the mud" (p. 265).

Album of Destiny was Jesse Stuart's third book of poetry. Coming ten years after *Man with a Bull-Tongue Plow,* it was to be his masterpiece. In spite of the fact that *Man with a Bull-Tongue Plow* gave him an identity as a writer, adverse criticisms of it fell heavily upon his ears. John Gould Fletcher, for example, found the book very displeasing:

> this modern Kentucky version of a folk-poet has apparently no previous models to go on. And so he has poured out all his feelings and experiences—trivial, interesting, important—into the mould of a single seven-hundred-times repeated form.

15. *Complete Poetry and Prose*, I, 77.
16. *Ibid.*, p. 67.

The result is monotony and blind confusion. This book, if it may be called such, lacking as it does all cohesion of plot, structure, or story, suffers from the same defect, but in a greater degree, as that which made *Spoon River Anthology* almost unendurable, and which defeated, in the end, Vachel Lindsay.[17]

Malcolm Cowley, who found much to praise in the book, also found that it had numerous faults:

Their worst fault [the poems] is that they are written without effort or economy. Jesse Stuart says everything at least twice. The lines come to him quickly and he sets them down as they come, without seeming to know the difference between the good and the bad ones, between the thoughts that are his own and those that have been expressed, not once before but ten thousand times, by every poetaster since the first bastard children of Homer.[18]

Listening to the critics' accusations that his book was too long, uneven, diffuse, and artless, Stuart was determined to do something about them. He would take his time, he thought, and produce a collection of poems which would please the critics. The idea for such a collection had come to him in 1932, two years before *Man with a Bull-Tongue Plow*.[19] As early as a year after publication of that book Stuart wrote that *Album of Destiny* was to have a definite plan, and he explained the plan in detail.[20] He worked on his book from 1932 until 1943, a definite contrast to the eleven months he had spent on *Man with a Bull-Tongue Plow*. Unwilling finally to rely on his own judgment, he was helped by Louise Townsend Nicholls, poet and editor for E. P. Dutton, and by

17. "Kentucky Georgics," *Poetry: A Magazine of Verse* 45 (1935), 218.
18. "Man with a Hoe," *The New Republic* 80 (1934), 342.
19. "Autobiographical Reminiscence," *University of Kansas City Review* 27 (October 1960), 61.
20. "Album of Destiny," *Literary America* 2 (1935), 490.

William Rose Benét, brother to Stephen Vincent Benét.[21] That help was not entirely a matter of judgment on the poet's part. He hurried to get the manuscript completed in 1943, before going into the navy, and it was largely because he was rushed that he lacked confidence in his own judgment. Consequently, he was given helpful critical suggestions concerning the closing poems of the collection. He actually read proofs while in the midst of basic training at Great Lakes Naval Training Center, near Chicago.

He was working against strange odds. A. E. (George W. Russell) had called *Man with a Bull-Tongue Plow* the greatest book of verse since *Leaves of Grass*,[22] but as Stuart himself pointed out, the critical consensus was that he had exhausted himself. "I have held their remarks in mind," he writes, "for ten years."[23] He knew that *Album of Destiny* had to be convincing. His reputation as a poet was on the line. Frank Leavell maintains that a survey of reviews shows that his poetry, by the time of *Album of Destiny*, had steadily declined in the eyes of the critics;[24] and although Leavell dismisses the reason as a matter of conjecture, it appears to be quite clear. Between *Man with a Bull-Tongue Plow* and *Album of Destiny* there were two collections of short stories—*Head O' W-Hollow* and *Men of the Mountains*. Only a year before the publication of *Album of Destiny*, and four years after his first novel, *Trees of Heaven*, he published a very successful novel, *Taps for Private Tussie*. This novel was a Book-of-the-Month Club selection, and also won the Thomas Jefferson Southern Award.[25] For many people, Jesse Stuart's reputation as a writer was, and still is, identified with that novel. The inescapable fact is that he had been reevaluated by the critics, and that they had

---

21. Letter to the writer, September 11, 1969.
22. Letter to Edwin Mims, December 2, 1939. Quoted in Ramey, p. 72.
23. "When Not to Take Advice," *Saturday Review of Literature* 28 (February 17, 1945), 11.
24. "The Literary Career of Jesse Stuart," p. 219.
25. See Hensley C. Woodbridge, *Jesse and Jane Stuart: A Bibliography* (Murray, Kentucky, 1969), p. xv.

found him to be a better novelist and story writer than he was a poet. Stuart knew this while he was preparing *Album of Destiny.* That what he considered to be his best book of poetry followed so closely the publication of a successful novel was perhaps unfortunate for a man who thought of himself as a poet.

Unwilling to accept the critics' opinions twelve years after *Album of Destiny* was published, he tried to defend his book in an article. The defense ends with weak rationalizing about why his work failed to impress the critics. Much of the reason, he argues, was that the war had produced a paper shortage, resulting in limited space for reviews. Unwilling to relent in his opinion, he cites Robert Hillyer's praise of the book as evidence of its success.[26] His "whole panorama of life," he concludes, impressed only a few reviewers, and his "strong, healthy brain-child grew weary shortly after birth."[27]

As the poet explains, the idea for *Album of Destiny* came to him while he was leafing through an old family album. The photographs moved him deeply; he was impressed by the way time had changed everyone. This, he recalls, was the idea for his next collection. He would take these people, begin with photographs of them in the springtime of their lives, and write portraits of them in verse. The lives he would divide into four parts to correspond to the seasons of the year, and he would show what happened in the spring, summer, fall, and winter of existence. This is essentially what he did. He used fifty people, and the names of all of them came from within Greenup County, Kentucky. He took them from newspapers and tombstones. He wrote four portraits for every one that was finally published, and sometimes he wrote as many as ten to get the right ones. He wrote them while traveling in Europe, and in at least forty different states in this country. He did more than 2000 portraits, and finally published 423.[28]

26. "Why I Think *Album* Is My Best," *Prairie Schooner* 30 (1956), 36.
27. *Ibid.*
28. *Ibid.*, p. 34.

Ruel Foster, in his book on Stuart, makes some interesting comments about both *Man with a Bull-Tongue Plow* and *Album of Destiny.* Death, he proposes, is the central theme of the former. There is a constant awareness, he adds, that death conquers all. He is quite right when he says that Stuart is not coy about man's going back to earth, back to a naturalistic end.[29] Favoring *Man with a Bull-Tongue Plow,* and largely for its spontaneity, he is willing to dismiss *Album of Destiny* as being too self-conscious, as a failure in modulating in different keys of emotion, and as a fundamental failure in diction.[30] Except for the charge of being overly self-conscious, the criticisms are about the same as those leveled against *Man with a Bull-Tongue Plow* ten years earlier. They, therefore, likely do not explain the success of the one book or the failure of the other. Foster, as the reviewers and critics did when *Album of Destiny* was published, is comparing successes and failures in different genres. He writes, for example, that Stuart can use his native idiom well in the short story but not so well in the poem.[31] What such an evaluation may mean, considering that Foster's primary interest is in prose, is that he fails to view *Album of Destiny* as the working out of an impasse (the finality of death) with which Stuart ended *Man with a Bull-Tongue Plow.*

By way of contrast, Frank Leavell considers *Album of Destiny* the most unjustifiably neglected book Stuart has written—"possibly his best book in any genre."[32] Leavell believes that it is more polished and has greater structural unity than most, if not all, of the poet's other books. The structural unity, he explains, is achieved through a system of symbols. Stuart agrees:

> I used in the prelude to this book certain symbols. I used the grass, wind, turtle, terrapin, poisonous and non-poisonous snake, water-dog and lizard. I used each for a certain symbol. I tried to portray the whole. In the

29. *Jesse Stuart* (New York, 1968), p. 61.
30. *Ibid.*, p. 67.
31. *Ibid.*
32. "The Literary Career of Jesse Stuart," p. 208.

epilogue, when I closed this span of living, I returned to these symbols to make the whole complete.[33]

The individual symbols, in spite of what the poet says, are not made clear to the reader. Nor does he attempt to explain them in the essay from which the quotation comes. The most that can be said is that in a general way they do seem to serve collectively to "make the whole complete." Ruel Foster explains:

> To frame this study of time and man, Stuart provides a "Prologue" and an "Epilogue" to show the beginning of earth-time and the swell of America into the generations of the future. He gets his effect by allowing the natural world to speak—the grass, wind, snakes, scorpion, and lizard—the whole of earth which is so completely Jesse Stuart's own; but the saurians and reptiles are also symbols of evolutionary beginnings of life. Life and death and the inevitability of suffering and death are his great themes. The immortality that he offers is that through the children who carry on the work of their sires. His intent seems clear—this book is intended to be a great tragic paean—a spacious panorama of Man's vexed journey toward death on this earth. It is a vast and elemental and age-old theme—echoes of Ecclesiastes, Virgil, and Shakespeare roll through it.[34]

John and Kathaleen Sutton are Stuart's central characters. Their "little world" is a miniature of the "big world," and they are Everyman. About them the poet says: "I did another album of their resurrected spring. I portrayed their children to show how life passed from one generation to the next generation that had given it life."[35] In *Album of Destiny* he adjusts his vision. For the first time he can see far beyond death and decay.

In the first poem the voice is that of the Whispering

33. "Why I Think *Album* Is My Best," p. 34.
34. *Jesse Stuart*, pp. 65-66.
35. "Why I Think *Album* Is My Best," p. 34.

Grass, who sees John Sutton and his wife Kathaleen through
"April eyes of my green liquid stems!"[36] They are a fair couple,
reports the Whispering Grass, who are much in love with each
other and with life. Once John and Kathaleen have been in-
troduced, the Whispering Grass next introduces the saurians.
Then people and reptiles are brought together in the same
portrait:

> Fair Kathaleen and John who laugh and sing
> Will give to me their portion for my petals!
> Even, slow shell-protected terrapin
> Shall give my fibers strength, bone for my stems;
> I nurture everything but blowing wind,
> The lamps of Heaven and earth's buried dreams.
>
> (p. 17)

One learns that the saurians have battled each other from the
beginning of time, and that they, rather than having de-
stroyed eath other, have only changed or evolved. As saurians
they have always been, but as individuals they will join John
and Kathaleen in "liquid stems of grass." As in Whitman the
leaf or stem of grass becomes a symbol of the insignificant
which is as "big as any." It symbolizes deathless equality, and
becomes a key to the enigma of Divine Reality:

> The smallest sprout shows there really is no death,
> And if ever there was it led forward life,
>   and does not wait at the end to arrest it,
> And ceas'd the moment life appear'd.
>
> All goes onward and outward, nothing collapses,[37]

John Sutton knows, although there is a "knit of identity" and
a "breed of life," that the "living mass moves on" (p. 32).

Pantheism alone is not a sufficient explanation for the
theory of Being in *Album of Destiny*. As indicated in the first
poem, the grass nurtures everything except the "blowing

---

36. *Album of Destiny* (New York, 1944), p. 17. Further references to
AD included in the text.
37. *Complete Poetry and Prose*, I, 67.

wind," the "lamps of Heaven," and "earth's buried dreams" (p. 17). The Whispering Wind does not pass through the "liquid stems of grass." On the contrary, it symbolically connects or relates mortal existence to something eternal:

> The Hand that cut the varied flakes of snow
> And Brain that gave the Sun its living heat
> Were Hand and Brain that made me force, I know—
> His own immortal plaything at His feet
> To guide the destiny of life about Him.
>
> (p. 22)

For Whitman there is the existent or living self, and there is the Transcendent—form, union, plan, and eternal life.[38] They are distinguished by the "moment" and "eternity." For Stuart there is the "golden minute" and "destiny." He has Cief Didway say: "My friend, our span of life's a golden minute" (p. 133). Destiny is the flow, the ebb from before and after the golden minute, and into the future. Trueman Abdon describes it: "But all creation is a mystery, / This flow of life on earth's eternal stream" (p. 133). As Shan Powderjay explains, destiny is big: "As high as walls of blowing wind are high, / And as to depths, I know there is no end" (p. 164). That there is no end, the poet emphasizes elsewhere. For example, Robert Diesel speaks of these "minute things between us and the sun" (p. 142), and Certis Sutton compares the tracks or paths of snakes to the furrows or trails made by human beings. These furrows are in turn compared to the trails of stars across the sky (p. 211).

Certis Sutton, crawling upon his belly "like a snake," and watching "one of these stars" from the tall weeds, illustrates Stuart's scheme of Being. In the trail of the star across the sky he sees his own trail or furrow across the face of the earth. He sees, in effect, that there is plan, pattern. The three trails— those of snake, man, and star—correspond. For Walt Whitman there are "outlines."[39] For Jesse Stuart there are "pat-

38. *Ibid.*, p. 67.
39. *Ibid.*, p. 113.

terns": "Come Love, let us resign ourselves to patterns / We did not make; patterns we do not choose" (p. 127). John elsewhere says to his wife Kathaleen, "If I had made the plan, life would not change" (p. 167).

As the moment relates to eternity, the part must relate to the whole. V. K. Chari, in his assessment of Whitman, writes that the problem of the poet-mystic is to construct a cosmos out of this "multifarious mad chaos," and thereby achieve inner and outer unity. He quotes from the Upanishads: "The Whole is all That. The Whole is all This. The Whole is born out of the Whole. When the Whole is absorbed into the Whole the Whole alone remains."[40] There is only the "Whole" being absorbed into the "Whole," emphasizing that there are no degrees of importance in the Divine Plan. For Whitman, "There are but parts, any thing is but a part."[41] For Stuart, whether he·is what Chari calls a poet-mystic or not, there are but "parts" that make the "whole." Certis Sutton asks his mother, "Can you now feel yourself a part of it, / A part of milkweed bloom and sawbriar blossom?" (p. 212) As indicated by examples such as this, the part-whole relationship becomes a matter of distinguishing, not a matter of discriminating, making it important, therefore, for still another reason. One who distinguishes between and among part and whole, moment and destiny, and chaos and order, must first recognize intimate interrelationships. The living human being, as part and moment, because of these limitations, cannot see the whole. His is therefore a world of chaos; at least it appears to be. Order and destiny are infinite, outside both time and space.

Chari says that the Whitman of "Song of Myself" is the " 'child' who became part of the objects and of whom the objects became a part."[42] The mystical center of experience, he believes, is the self. Stuart's scorpion comments on selfhood:

My Lady Scorpion picked up dust of us

40. *Brihadaranyaka Upanishad*, 5.1. Quoted in *Whitman in the Light of Vedantic Mysticism* (Lincoln, Nebraska, 1964), pp. 54-55.
41. *Complete Poetry and Prose*, I, 108.
42. *Whitman in the Light of Vedantic Mysticism*, p. 56.

And held it for the wind to blow away.
She could not tell which dust was which of us,
For it was dust one color: it was gray—
The dusts of John, Gray Lizard, and of me
Mingle and blow through our eternity. (p. 129)

Here the poet uses Whitman's word "eternity." John is caught up with the saurians in the eternal flow. Kathaleen sees the flow as existing in "four full seasons of the sun," and resigns herself to the mystery, admitting that this "change of man may be for many reasons" (p. 127). There is, on the one hand, an endless succession of golden minutes or life-spans: "Birth of my twelve has been my resurrection!" (p. 172) On the other hand, there is the eternal flow of life: "For I shall be the growing leaf again / Soon as this templed clay has come undone" (p. 179). One hardly knows what to do with the "twelve" that crops up again. Perhaps it is intended to affirm the necessity of a Christian resurrection for the golden minute, the span of limited vision. Whether it is or not, there is always Whitman's "perpetual transfer" between the golden minutes and the eternal flow, the influx and efflux, the liquid stems of blades of grass.

The poet sees the destiny of America to be a matter of blood, a succession of golden minutes: "Are we not of the blood in our sires' veins?" (p. 210) Mortals come and go, but they must not close their eyes to the "beauty of death-world" (p. 126). Those in the "city of the dead" are to be envied rather than pitied (p. 237). Death, being "compounded under sprout and thyme" (p. 206), is luckier than one might think. The process of compounding is illustrated in the rotting down into the elements of Flem Spry's old house (p. 188). Everywhere there is life in the midst of decay—life, in Whitman's words, as the "leavings of many deaths."[43]

The scope of Jesse Stuart's ontological scheme is much more complicated and detailed. The purpose here, which is necessarily limited, has been to establish that there is such a

---

43. *Complete Poetry and Prose*, I, 112.

scheme, and to explain something of its genesis. As indicated earlier, *Beyond Dark Hills* is important because it is a sourcebook of origins. It contains early observations about such things as man, nature, death, religion, and God, and makes evident the poet's need for working out a philosophy of some kind. The working out of the philosophy is done through his first three volumes of verse, and Walt Whitman, as the model, becomes increasingly influential in each additional volume. Further, those who have criticized him for what appears to be his formlessness need look once again at Whitman. He was so impressed by Whitman's technique of symphonic development of theme that he borrowed it. Like Whitman, he develops a number of themes at one time. He moves from one to the other, but does not abandon them. Instead, each is cast aside and recalled at what appears to be the poet's convenience. One can learn much about both poets by reading Malcolm Cowley's Introduction to the Deathbed Edition of *Leaves of Grass*. He can learn, for instance, that Cowley's discussion of Whitman's faults contains virtually all of the faults that critics and reviewers found in Stuart up to and including *Album of Destiny.*

Harvest of Youth and *Man with a Bull-Tongue Plow* modulate between life and death. Each contains numerous examples of raw naturalism, and although the latter can be appreciated for its pantheistic impressions, death is final in both. Not until *Album of Destiny* does Stuart come full circle. To the life-death syndrome, the impasse with which he ends *Man with a Bull-Tongue Plow,* he offers a solution. In *Album of Destiny* he adjusts his vision and sees in terms of the whole. The book, notwithstanding, proved much too grave for the psychological moment. His readers were still laughing hilariously over the humor in *Taps for Private Tussie.* He was chagrined, to say the least, for *Album of Destiny* was his planned attempt to arrest his declining reputation as a poet. He had developed his "brain-child" with great care, but then the role of the philosopher-poet seems far removed from that of "a farmer singing at the plow." He was obviously out of character.

3

The Juvenilia: An Experiment in Form and Technique

T. S. Eliot viewed the Twenties and Thirties as a period in which poets were searching for a proper modern colloquial idiom.[1] Spearheaded by the Imagists, it was a time in which being a poet became synonymous with being a craftsman. Stuart, too, as indicated by his courtships in *Harvest of Youth* (and in spite of what he has said to the contrary), wanted to be a craftsman. He courted the writers of *vers libre,* the Imagists, the Symbolists, the Traditionalists, and other groups. His courtships were legion, but none of them lasted. When he came home from Vanderbilt in 1932 he had decided, in fact, to end the courtship for craft: "I decided to be what I am."[2] Blair writes: "The young Stuart [the Stuart of *Harvest of Youth*] experimented lavishly with verse forms with results that were interesting and sometimes dramatic."[3] There is little doubt that he was searching for his own idiom, and he finally found it in the speech of the people in W-Hollow and the surrounding area. One sees in the poet's juvenilia an early beginning at

1. "The Music of Poetry," *On Poetry and Poets* (New York, 1957), p. 32.
2. Letter to Ruel Foster, May 17, 1963. Quoted in *Jesse Stuart* (New York, 1968), p. 54.
3. *Jesse Stuart: His Life and Works* (Columbia, South Carolina, 1967), p. 68.

trying to strike some kind of functional balance between the forms of tradition and the speech patterns of his people.

Because some of the work in *Harvest of Youth* goes back to when Stuart was sixteen, one can hardly expect it to show outstanding accomplishment. What it does show is something of the seriousness with which the young poet experimented. The first poem in the collection was surely inspired by E. A. Robinson's "House on the Hill":

House on the Hill

What's become of the house on the hill?
Weeds choke the corn; the garden's dead;
The burdock grows at the rotting sill;
Smart weeds grow in the tulip bed
Life too has grown curiously still
Since something is wrong on the hill.

Last spring we knew how Lucy kept
The yards alive, the hedge in trim,
The garden clean, the walkways swept,
And how she did the chores for him
Who worked till nine before he slept:
The way man passes time unwept.

Now John is dead since Lucy died.
Once things went well and he went right,
But then he wed the other bride
Who snarls him with her subtile might.
He never says a gay good-night,
He pauses time in moody light.

She grew so wily she would dare
To go to town and go alone
With Lucy's tulips in her hair.
Since she had now some bolder grown
John sat at home and sat alone
Obeying her defiant tone.

She thought that Lucy's ways were vain.

What Lucy did she would not do.
She found his faults with much disdain;
He lost heart trying, lost her too:
His fate was near. He fell into
Strange company and careless grew.

While now he drinks to drown his care;
One life he thinks—I live today—
He dreams of her in the old house there
A girl so different to his way.
Strange to think people would say:
"He'll be alright with her away."

Here's what's wrong with the house on the hill:
Why the corn's unkept and the garden dead;
Why burdock grows at the rotting sill;
Why smart weeds grow in the tulip bed;
The saloon is his desire for ill
Since her white body haunts him still. (pp. 13-14)

At least four things which are evident here become important
to the poet later. First, the heavy end-stopping becomes
characteristic of his treatment of the line. Second, as in the
first two lines, the sentence and the line often correspond. And
third, the center of the line is used, with the last half often
consisting of a modifying clause or phrase. Finally, the stanza
indicates something of the importance of rhyme to Stuart's
early verse. A stanzaic analysis of "House on the Hill" shows
rhyme to be regular. The pattern used is ABABBB. All
rhymes in "House on the Hill" are masculine. A preponder-
ance of monosyllables tends to force the poet to rhyme the last
stressed syllable, which in his case is usually the last word in
the line.

The remainder of the poems in the first section of *Harvest
of Youth*—except "Lilac Elegy," "Sleep," and "For Warriors
Dead"—are all written in quatrains. "What There Is to an Old
House" is written in four-three measure, and the rhyme
scheme is ABAB. It probably is not regular enough to be con-
sidered common measure, and the repetends, along with the

refrain,[4] convince the reader that the poet is trying the stanza form that Coleridge used in "The Rime of the Ancient Mariner." He is, in effect, trying the literary ballad.

The first section of poems in *Harvest of Youth* is entitled "Out of the Night." And although it strains for an elegiac tone, nowhere is there convincing evidence of a debt to W. E. Henley. The second section is entitled "Slabs from a Sun-Down World," concerning which the poet has many times admitted his debt to Sandburg. The poems in the second section have little in common with those in the first:

River Railroad Man

Shovel under this old river railroad man with
    reverence.
He slept river nights of his life working
After days of work on river railroads.
Now he goes to his long sleep.
Still, heavy trains sweep on to their destiny
For his life is in them and lives.
His blood is in the smoke.
His blood is in the steel.
He heard mean winds strike the cold wiring on
    zero mornings.
And whistle through the lonesome tree trops.
He heard moaning engines climb steep river grades
And he heard the click of steel battering steel.
Now these same sounds that once he heard
Will continue to whine over his cool tomb
Where he will lie cold
And dream of picks and shovels. (p. 27)

Although "River Railroad Man" appears at first glance to amount to so much prose, it is not so formless as it looks. It is

---

4. The distinction is that the repetend consists of a partial repetition of a word, phrase, or clause, but not in a predetermined place. The refrain, on the other hand, repeats a whole line or combination of lines in a predetermined place.

doubly important, along with other poems in this section, because it shows the poet exploring techniques which are unrelated to counting syllables—techniques which eventually become a part of his mature work.

One does not have to look far to realize that the idea and the form were inspired by Carl Sandburg. Nevertheless, when one holds "River Railroad Man"up to "Cool Tombs," and at the same time holds "House on the Hill" up to Robinson's poem, he is more than ever convinced that *Harvest of Youth* is genuinely and sincerely experimental. The young poet is trying different modes, is working out different effects, and is allowing himself much latitude in exploring idiom. In the case of "Cool Tombs," and in "House on the Hill," he borrows an idea along with an occasional phrase. His work is heavily influenced by the tone of the poet who is inspiring him, but in both cases he writes his own poem. In fact, he creates a new situation, a new set of circumstances, and what he does with them is peculiarly his.

Prior to examining Stuart's major technical problems, one should look closely at some of the poems in "Sonnets: Juvenilia," the third section of *Harvest of Youth*. Collectively, they represent the beginning of a career as sonnet writer. Exercises in what Eliot calls "making the pattern comply," they contain all of the problems which characterize later poems, and some of the virtues. Rhyme, for instance, has always been troublesome for the poet's readers, as have diction and idiom. They are intricately related to subject matter—to a time, a place, and a people. As far as criticism is concerned, formalism appears to be helpful but inadequate and this in spite of the fact that considerable attention must be paid to form. The intentional fallacy (falling back on the writer's intentions) and the affective fallacy (falling back on the reader's emotional response) seem almost necessary if one is to appreciate Jesse Stuart. Formalism remains hostile to the historical method, but he who criticizes the W-Hollow poet either will have to acknowledge the historical approach or throw up his hands in despair. In any given situation, answers to questions concerning what he does are closely related to why he does it. Singular answers are seldom satisfying.

In the young poet's experimental sonnets, one finds the rhyme scheme which he finally settled for:

Loneliness

I still remember when you went away
On that red morning in the summer drouth,
When dry winds blew from out the lonely south;
I still remember all you had to say.
Vines then that draped the cottage wall
Have turned buff colored in the sun;
Beech leaves are slowly dropping one by one;
And south-going birds only stop to call.
The loneliness and Life's little things bring back
You to me again. The ghosts of autumn rains
Tapping the roof, beating the window panes,
Gambling with Night's deserted waste of black,
I cannot forget. My life is lost in you
As azure skies are lost in windless blue.

(HY, p. 47)

One readily sees much to criticize—the Victorian personifications in "Life's" and "Night's," the cliché "azure skies," and the sameness of sounds in the rhymes. Looking beyond these faults, one sees that the rhyme scheme—ABBA, CDDC, EFFE, GG—conforms to a pattern consisting of three brace stanzas and a couplet. As a formula, the poet employs it extensively in *Man with a Bull-Tongue Plow* and *Album of Destiny*.

That Stuart deliberately set out to resurrect the sonnet as a form is in itself interesting. American writers, until the last two or three decades, have treated form as grammarians watching over their rules and insisting that they not be broken. The advent of modern linguistics—insisting on describing what is and prescribing nothing—has had a great impact on shaping attitudes toward language as literary medium, and as Rene Wellek and Austin Warren indicate, toward the whole idea of form.[5] Eliot, too, has had noteworthy influence. In his essay "The Music of Poetry" he recognizes what he calls the "inner unity" of the poem as unique and the "outer unity" as typical. Forms, he contends, have to be broken and remade because language is always changing. Eliot sees a necessity for returning to set patterns and forms, but always for the purpose of pulling away. "In a perfect sonnet," he believes, "what you admire is not so much the author's skill in adapting himself to the pattern as the skill and power with which he makes the pattern comply with what he has to say."[6]

Be that as it may, Stuart's reasons for writing sonnets remain, and after reading hundreds of them one suspects that he avoids talking about the most important reason, or that he has never fully understood it. In any event, one has to begin with the intensive search for form which begins in *Harvest of Youth* and culminates in *Album of Destiny*. He must accept that the poet is anachronistic, and that the "old way of life" which he holds constantly before the reader is cherished principally for what it is, or possibly for what the poet makes of it. The old way is simplistic, and it contains a recognizable value system. It is orderly. And although accepting or rejecting the order is left to the reader, it is always there—in the seasons of the year, in the lifespan of the individual, and in the evolution of the race from the time of the saurians which are so much a part of *Album of Destiny*. The poet sees order in the birth of a bud, in the falling of a leaf, in the rising and setting of the sun, and in the rhythmic beating of a heart, as he discusses it in *The Year of My Rebirth*. In this autobiography, more than anywhere else, one is told that God in the very beginning ordained an orderly universe, as though it is an admission that the poet had looked forward to making throughout his career.

Like other writers of his time, Jesse Stuart feels that he is alienated from the world at large. Also like other writers, he

5. See particularly Chapter 12, "The Mode of Existence of a Literary Work of Art," and Chapter 17, "Literary Genres," in *Theory of Literature* (New York, 1956).
6. *On Poetry and Poets*, pp. 30-31.

constantly attempts to reclaim the world, but on his own terms. In an essay entitled "The Problem of Form," J. V. Cunningham states the matter with considerable accuracy.[7] He argues that we are a democratic society which values informality, and which consequently will have nothing to do with formal language and figures or rhetoric, because such things belong to authoritarian societies in which ceremony and formality are conducive to a way of life. The attitudes which foster informality and antiformality, he continues, are concomitants of democratic revolution, which in turn is a concomitant of the nineteenth-century romantic revolution. Hence, he concludes, the "measured, the formal, the contrived, the artificial are, we feel, insincere; they are perversions of the central value of our life."[8] In other words, the problem of form is peculiarly ours because we praise what we prefer to call the real, often disregarding how vulgar it is. About the problem of form in poetry in particular, Cunningham writes:

> We have lost the repetitive harmony of the old tradition, and we have not established a new. We have written to vary or violate the old line, for regularity we feel is meaningless and irregularity meaningful. But a generation of poets, acting on the principles and practice of significant variation, have at last nothing to vary from. The last variation is regularity.[9]

To get rid of form, he insists, we must keep it, for there must always be something to rid oneself of.

Paul Fussell, Jr., views the problem of form similarly. He, too, sees it as a matter of attitudes and values reflecting the history of a culture:

> something important has happened to the poet's posture toward received poetic forms . . . the contemporary poet,

---

7. See *The Problem of Style*, ed. J. V. Cunningham (Greenwich, Connecticut, 1966), pp. 277-280.
8. *Ibid.*, p. 278.
9. *Ibid.*, p. 280.

anxious to escape from the fixed forms, is conducting his own small skirmish in the continuing romantic and democratic revolutions. But a poetry without a memory of its fixed forms . . . abandons a dimension of meaning that it simply cannot afford to lose.[10]

Because the poem is an expression of experience, it seems, the modern poet cannot write in fixed forms. Although such forms were once useful, they reflect attitudes that are alien to our time and place in history. In his summary of the problem, Fussell finds no acceptable solution:

The challenge to contemporary poetry is a pair of unhappy alternatives; either to continue certain schemes of empirically meaningful repetition that reflect and—more importantly—transmit the color of contemporary experience; or to recover schemes that have reflected the experience of the past. To do the first would be to imply that contemporary experience has a pattern, a point that most post-Christian thinkers would deny. To do the second would be to suggest that the past can be recaptured, to suggest that the intolerable fractures and dislocations of modern history have not really occurred at all, or, what is worse, to suggest that they may have occurred but that poetry should act as if they have not. Between these two demands of accuracy of registration, on the one hand, and aesthetic organization, on the other, we seem to find no technique of reconciliation.[11]

Stuart, fully aware of the problem of form and its alternatives, has found his own solution. He uses forms from the past, as his sonnets indicate, and through them creates a past to his own liking. By employing an isolated part of the country for subject matter, he can do that and in the process remain more convincing than writers with less restricted subjects. Through his memory of "the good old days," he reclaims a past which will allow him to reflect what he would like to see in

10. *Poetic Meter and Poetic Form* (New York, 1965), p. 163.
11. *Ibid.*, p. 164.

experience of the present. And although he agrees with post-Christian thinkers about loss of order and meaning, he refuses to accept the idea that there can never again be an organized existence. Such a view may amount to little more than foolish optimism and naiveté, but it has allowed the poet a means of surviving in an otherwise hostile and chaotic world.

Any writer can probably find a way to appreciate the observations of Cunningham and Fussell concerning the interreliance of a culture and its art forms. When one has read them, he comes away feeling that he agrees, even though they are both lacking in sufficient examples to warrant their generalizations. But one need not accept unsupported generalizations. To be sure, there are examples—some of which are based on the most traumatic experiences of our time. For instance, Donald Hassler, a professor in English at Kent State University in Ohio, witnessed the controversial shootings which took place there on May 4, 1970. Almost a year later, in April of 1971, he read some of his poems at the annual meeting of the Ohio Poets' Association in Ashland, Ohio. He began by announcing that for the first time in many years he had tried to write sonnets, and apologetically explained his poems as what he called "one poet's attempt to return to order in a time that of all times needs a sense of tradition and order."[12] Viewing the horror surrounding the shootings as symptomatic of a national illness, he read "May 4, 1970":

> We have wasted our lives as James Wright said
> He did on bookish matters. We are lost
> in John Barth's funhouse. Design of Robert Frost
> Has been our creed, and now four kids are dead.
> We talk too much. Our wives have learned to dread
> The nights of mental exercise. The cost
> May be too great as wrinkled sheets are tossed
> Away for waste, and now four kids are dead.
> But what else could we do? The sonnet form
> Won't let us drive our horses roughly shod

---

12. Taken from my personal notes, dated April 17, 1971.

Or bull our way through virgin fields of hay.
Analysis is all that we can lay
Against the darkness and an absent God.
We save what we can in a wasting storm.[13]

The shootings are always in the poet's mind, as indicated in the refrain, for they are overwhelming evidence of the darkness, and that God is absent. The reference to the sonnet form, needless to say, bears heavily upon the problem of old forms which will not fit a new way of life.

Hopefully, the digression of the last few pages is warranted. It is intended as an elaboration upon—and a clarification of—a problem which Jesse Stuart has grappled with for many years. He could have borrowed his dedication to the sonnet from anyone, the most likely of whom is Merrill Moore, who was at Vanderbilt when the poet was there. When asked about Moore, though, Stuart responded with this: "Merrill Moore didn't influence me. I met him only once, a very delightful man, and he suggested to me that I send sonnets to *Dublin Review,* Dublin, Ireland. I did and four were accepted."[14] The sonnets in *Harvest of Youth* indicate that Moore could never have been other than a latent influence; the form worked out there has continued in all of the poet's collections. No, the sonnet that he developed did not come from having read any one poet, although he read Shakespearian, Spenserian, and Italian sonnets in high school and college. The form fitted his needs and his method; there is little to say beyond that.

Even though the experimental sonnets in *Harvest of Youth* constitute the best of the juvenilia, one can hardly expect them to be fully successful poems. Experiments are important because they identify a direction and often lead to something better. This appears to be the case with Jesse Stuart. He did not discard what he learned about repeating and paralleling in his free-verse experiments. One finds in the

---

13. *Read Out, Read In,* ed. Richard Snyder and Robert McGovern (Ashland, Ohio, 1971), p. 15.
14. Letter to the writer, March 27, 1972.

sonnets numerous examples of repeating a pattern, and parallels are equally plentiful:

> They see my eyes heavy-lidded, wet with dreams;
> They see my candle soul send forth its beams
> > ("My Mountain Home," p. 50)

> Not mine the clean white robes that angels wear:
> Not mine the stern oblivious paradise . . .
> > ("Heaven Enough," p. 54)

> Can you remember a dread that banished?
> A love that faded . . . a joy that vanished?
> > ("To Edith," p. 49)

For convincing evidence of successful repetitions one should look at "To Edith," in which "Do you remember" comes at the beginning of lines one and four, near the end of seven, and changes to "Can you remember" at the beginning of thirteen. He should also look at them in "Heaven Enough" (p. 54), in "It Will Not Matter Much" (p. 55), and in "The Wind Has Ways" (p. 55). In each case they successfully lend structural unity to the entire poem.

In some of the experiments there is an obvious attempt to isolate and repeat specific vowels and consonants, although the poet prefers to repeat individual sounds embedded in larger units and thereby avoid any possibility that the sounds will call attention to themselves. "The crow's deep clarion call," in "Personae" (p. 59), is an exception, but here he is exploring ways of holding a twelve-syllable line together. More typically one sees something like this, in which the structure is obviously archaic: "They fight, they drive, flinch not, for they are unafraid" ("Two Lives," p. 57). Sometimes the predominant sound exists both in and out of repeated words and their derivatives:

> Like some deep singer in the voiceless you fling
> Futility to wind and march and sing and sing,
> > ("To Muddy Waters," p. 54)

In "Returned" he also experiments with holding a twelve-syllable line together and finds that alliteration is one way of doing it:

> To visit *f*avorite haunts, to *f*amiliar *f*aces,
> Live now as I did then and *f*eel at least as *f*ree. (p. 52)

Something is obviously missing from the last half of the first line; balance alone demands an insertion there.

In the first section of *Harvest of Youth,* the poet experiments with writing verses, and in the second he experiments with prosodic techniques. He brings the results together and experiments with writing poetry in the third. In the fourth and last, though, he falls back on his exercises in writing the quatrain. One can only conjecture about why he ends his collection by going back to the exercises conducted in the first two sections. The poems may simply have been earlier ones added to make a few more pages. On the other hand, he gave the last section the same title that he gave the book: "Harvest of Youth." It is possible that he considered the final poems to be his best, although it is more probable that he knew he was not ready to write with distinction, and therefore returned to the early experiments to explore ways of improving them.

Either way, one encounters many disappointments in reading Stuart's juvenilia, and some of the problems found there have remained with him. Diction is a case in point. One can easily assume that the poet does not know clichés and archaisms when he sees them. The alternative is to accept that he not only knows, but that he actively cultivates them. If one finds the explanation to lie in ignorance, he can quickly dismiss the poetry as faulty. If he chooses to believe that the poet is reasonably knowledgeable about matters of language, on the contrary, he is obligated to look further for possible solutions. To be sure, the exactness of a measurement does not depend entirely upon the thing being measured. Two other issues are extremely vital. One is the appropriateness of the tools being used, and the other is the competence of the person doing the measuring. Still, when the job of measuring has been completed, one may still want to dismiss Stuart's diction as faulty, but then he is justified—because he knows why.

The terms "diction" and "idiom" are frequently used interchangeably, for both have to do with means and manner in expressing ideas. In one sense, "diction" refers to style as dependent upon choice of words, and "idiom" to constructions or expressions peculiar to a language. When a writer attempts to represent the language habits of a people, as Stuart does, the two become closely identified. Considered together or apart, they have always posed difficulty for his readers, and because of that deserve special attention. Ruel Foster has recognized something of the gravity of the problem:

> Although Louise Cowan remarked that Jesse Stuart lacked the "pietas" of Southern poetry ["The 'Pietas' of Southern Poetry," *South: Modern Southern Literature in Its Cultural Setting,* Rubin and Jacobs, ed. (New York, 1961), p. 99], this statement seems manifestly untrue. Stuart does have the "pietas," but lacks the grace of idiom to convey it justly. Why Stuart can use the idiom in the short story and not in the poem is difficult to answer— perhaps inexplicable, even to him.[15]

Presumably, Foster means by "idiom" the poet's selection of expressions and how they are used. Whether in fiction or prose, words must be both effective and appropriate—a style of speaking peculiar to the language of a people. "Pietas," too, has a built-in concern for appropriateness. The Roman idea of reverence before the gods and one's ancestors had to be spoken and acted out in socially acceptable ways. Maintaining a sense of respect is not merely a question of deeds. It is also one of corresponding verbal behavior.

The matter of appropriateness has always been complicated for Stuart, and rightly so. Because his writing is anachronistic, his diction is frequently archaic. And since he relies heavily upon the first-person point of view—usually an uneducated hill dweller as spokesman—his fiction and poems contain many clichés. His sense of awe for things which are

---

15. *Jesse Stuart,* p. 67.

uncontrollable and often inexplicable—life, death, God, sin, the devil, and nature—early resulted in Victorian personifications which continue in much of what he writes. Paul Engle has put it this way: "Ignoring all of the frequent modern manners in verse—the irony, the elusive reference, the subtleties of implication, the startling images—he has chosen to keep the traditional ways."[16] Everetta Love Blair sees the issue of language quite differently. For her, it is not so much a matter of choice as one of time and place:

> In Jesse Stuart's works, which cover his region's transition from a remote area, repository of early Anglo-Saxon customs and language, to an area now responding to the influence of good roads, scientific farming, better schools and television, and falling into the pattern of modern life, there is careful attention to use of vestigial words and expressions, as well as to the use of current vernacular.
>
> At the turn of the twentieth century, the vernacular of the Kentucky hill people still showed a strong flavor of Chaucerian and seventeenth and eighteenth century usage.[17]

Mary Washington Clarke agrees that the poet is faithful in his task of trying to represent idiom which is in a rapid state of transition: "Stuart goes all the way, faithfully presenting the anachronisms, irregularities, and paradoxes of an antique speech caught up in rapid shift toward modernity."[18] The poet has always been aware of the rapidity of change, and the implications which it has for the writer: "We have, perhaps, changed more than any other regional segment of America. There isn't any dialect left with our youngsters. . . . Now we are just about like every other community in America."[19] His attitude toward the appropriate word, nonetheless, was ex-

16. "Over the Mountain," *The New York Times*, September 1, 1963, sec. 7, p. 5.
17. *Jesse Stuart: His Life and Works*, p. 14.
18. *Jesse Stuart's Kentucky* (New York, 1968), p. 1.
19. "America's Last Carbon Copy," *Saturday Review* 40 (December 28, 1957), p. 5.

pressed as early as the autobiographical *Beyond Dark Hills*. There he relates an incident about a girl who is frustrated when she talks to her teacher. She can not decide whether to use "ring," "rang," or "rung" in explaining her being late getting to school. Writing about it later, the poet muses: "I thought that was funny. She was afraid of three words. I would just say one. What did it matter, right or wrong? I wouldn't be afraid, at least."[20]

About diction and idiom in general, two issues stand in need of further clarification—Ruel Foster's contention that "grace of idiom" is more central to the poems than to the fiction, and the question of appropriateness for a modern audience. In a large way, the first of these is explicable as a result of its being conducive to the poet's first-person technique. In the prose, characterization and speech are closely related. One, two, three, or more characters are held in the mind and written about long enough to allow idiosyncrasies of speech to accumulate. Subsequently, the accuracy of any one expression can be worked out in context by holding it up to others coming from the same character. Such is not the case with the poems. The sonnet form is extremely restricted, and as the poet flits from one to another he also moves from one voice to another—ultimately through hundreds of them in *Man with a Bull-Tongue Plow* and *Album of Destiny*. He might have exercised more control had he sustained one voice throughout a succession of poems, but he did not choose to do that. Instead, he picks them up and drops them at random. And although the rapid succession of voices is probably not the only explanation for what Foster calls a failure in diction, it is an important one. As in *Man with a Bull-Tongue Plow,* there are too many voices—partially because the poet's plan allows for little consistency, and also because he lets everyone from the unborn child to the long-dead grandfather have his say.

The second issue, that of appropriateness for a modern audience, is equally difficult. In spite of what Jesse Stuart says about the rapid changes which have taken place in his part of Appalachia, he has never accepted them. He has verbalized his opposition to being overcivilized and overindustrialized. His attitude was put on display publicly while he was a visiting professor at American University in Cairo, Egypt (1960-1961). Disturbed by the encroachment of modern civilization upon Egyptian villages, he made a plea in the name of poetry: "I put before the government of this country my pathetic appeal to stop modern technological advancement from destroying the poetic nature of Egyptian villages."[21] Frank Leavell, in his dissertation, interprets the poet's charge to the Egyptian government as real evidence of his refusal to accept the coming of material progress to his own Appalachian hill country.[22] Leavell's assessment of the poet's attitude is accurate. Both the fiction and the poems are about the "old way." In his most recent collections of poems —*Kentucky Is My Land* (1952) and *Hold April* (1962)— modernity is still conspicuously missing. In his even more recent stories—*Dawn of Remembered Spring* (1972)—W-Hollow remains an isolated frontier world, and the language belongs to those who people it. The problem arises, as it inevitably must, in the poet's attempt to bridge the gap which exists between that world and the present one. Although the language of the stories and the poems may be historically accurate, it has long been forgotten by those who once knew it. Furthermore, young America is peopled by a generation of city dwellers who have never heard it, except for those in a few isolated sections. Appropriateness for the speaker or character is one thing, but appropriateness for the audience is quite another. It remains a crucial problem for Jesse Stuart—one which he will have to give even greater attention in the future.

Another problem one finds in the poet's juvenilia, which persists in all of his collections, is that of rhyme. Again, the question of ignorance applies. But assuming that he knows

---

20. See *Beyond Dark Hills* (New York, 1938), p. 49.
21. "Stuart Faces a Hard Task in Cairo," *Campus Caravan,* February 13, 1961. Quoted in Frank Leavell, "The Literary Career of Jesse Stuart" (Unpublished Ph.D. dissertation, Vanderbilt University, 1965), p. 170.
22. "The Literary Career of Jesse Stuart," p. 170.

how out of vogue his rhymes are, there must be explanations other than the usual canned ones. There are many peculiarities in literary analysis, and one of them is that we object to received form, and to formulas and techniques tried by time. Meanwhile, we insist upon using received techniques of analysis. We cultivate our intuition, and look for answers in what we call aesthetics. But taste, too, has its reasons—which are largely temporal and spatial. One's acquisitions depend heavily upon what he is exposed to, and not necessarily upon the exposure of others. Common exposure, presumably, will get similarity of taste. In the final analysis, we frequently hear each other discussing "the poem," indicative of the extent to which we have come to accept an archetypal poetry. And although the archetype may stand as adequate yardstick for what is, we have forgotten the history behind its evolution. In other words, the archetype pulls toward a center which has lost its reason for being.

Admittedly, it may be presumptuous to write about rhyme in our day; practitioners of open form flatly deny that it can have any intrinsic value. Possessing a psyche geared toward individual liberation from all restraint, and a psychology of phenomenological analysis, we are probably not equipped to assess confinement, even in an aesthetic sense. We seem overly eager to detest rhyme, though memory reminds us that we were brought up on it. Paradoxically, having been brought up on it has made us even more confidently adamant in our denunciations. It could be that our attitudes toward rhyme in particular reflect our attitudes toward form in general, which in turn says something about what we find to have meaning in life, and about where we place our values. We know eighteenth century neoclassicism and nineteenth century romanticism, but we see ourselves as far removed from either. Most probably, ours remains the dark, deep void of the existentialist. At least the gnawing pessimism which surrounds us would indicate that such is the case. But we seem to delight in being in the dark, in not knowing. One even wonders whether we are masochistic, causing us to delight in not being—especially if the term means needing reason or rational explanation for perpetuating the life of the individual, or that of the species. Indeed, it seems quite obvious that rhyme has no place in a world such as ours. It belongs to an ordered existence, one which has balance, symmetry, and harmony. As a consequence, American prosodists have largely ignored the discussion of rhyme in the twentieth century. And even in the few efforts to treat it which do exist, it is handled as degree of mere likeness in word sounds accompanied by an occasional catalogue of approximations. Reduced to an examination of sonic value, and at the same time ignoring semantic and aesthetic value, such treatises have failed to make clear why it is inherently bad or inappropriate. Received opinions aside, rhyme is a central and often glaring fact in the poetry of Jesse Stuart.

No one has attempted an analysis of the poet's rhymes, nor has Stuart tried to justify them. When he speaks of them, he is almost always referring to poetry or the process of writing it. For him, rhyme becomes synonymous with the poem, and writing with the process of composing. He frequently refers to "spinning" or "making" rhymes. Still, near the end of *Man with a Bull-Tongue Plow* there are brief references which cause one to be curious about how deliberately they are worked out. About words he says: "I rhymed them to the slow beat of a drum / And to the whirs of dead leaves drifting down" (p. 348). This could suggest that the sounds of the words are timed by some event in the poet's experience, and possibly determined by it. Another of the sonnets intimates that rhyme is a rhetorical consideration:

> Maybe there is the sound of windless rain,
> The steady thump of rain on my grave rock;
> I have no way to tell with this dead brain
> The sound of rain that's ticking like a clock.
> Though flesh is close related to the time;
> (My ears are deaf to any ticking sound)
> Though life is close related to the rhyme;
> What chance has one now lying under ground?

And then to think each comes and takes his turn.
Each man's a god and each is crucified—
Each goes back to the dirt and grass and fern
After the temple of his flesh has died.
Each comes and goes and each must go alone;
Each life is dirt and time and rhyme and stone.

(p. 348)

Viewing the lines in the context of his concept of the image, and keeping in mind his concept of the poem as poem, one finds ample justification for weighing rhyme as rhetorical device.

In line seven above, life is "close related to the rhyme," and the process of coming into and going out of it is made clear in the idea of crucifixion. God, too, took on flesh and became a man. Like Him, "each man comes and takes his turn," but in the framework of the old life-death-resurrection ritual pattern, it is life which the poet emphasizes—the time in which a man has identity apart from "dirt and grass and fern." In one sense it is a punctuation mark signaling the end of one rhythmic cycle of existence and the beginning of another; one man dies and another is born. Further, one should be cautious in placing singular emphasis upon Hebrew religion; all religions have gods who conform to the same pattern. Certainly, the parallels of Hebrew poetry are exceptions to the idea of rhyme proposed here. On the other hand, the German philosopher-poet Johann Gottfried von Herder (1744-1803) found a similar explanation for it in oriental parallelism. It comes, he contended, from the artistic method of expressing nature as balanced dualities—life and death, heaven and earth, love and hate, good and evil. Repetition of any event creates balance, and a succession leads to harmony. Rhyme, therefore, is progressive parallelism, suggests Herder, consisting of a symmetrical correspondence of lines. The explanation lies in having a body *and* a soul, a right side *and* a left.[23]

According to principles of Greek rhetoric, the end of an

---

23. For a summary of Herder's position, see Henry Lanz, *The Physical Basis of Rime* (Stanford University, 1931), p. 183.

event—given any temporal unit—is the most interesting.
And as rhetoric handbooks show, events are placed in a dis-
course subject to their interest value. Numerically, they can
be labelled two, three, one. Paul Fussell, Jr., has elaborated on
the importance of this to the poet:

> In this one important way the poet's formal problem is
> very close to the prose writer's, for the poetic line, regard-
> less of its degree of syntactical integrity, is like a prose
> sentence, or an opera, or a footrace in being an experience
> in time and in sharing in the emphasis pattern which
> characterizes all such experiences.[24]

If Fussell is correct, historically considered, rhyme is the basic
element of coherence in the stanza or strophe, and the pat-
terning or cohering of lines into stanzas determines the
character of the poem.

Experiments in *Harvest of Youth* include rhyme. And al-
though treating it without discussing meter, syntax, alliitera-
tion, assonance, and other tonal devices is awkward, a few
examples should be adequate to show the range of experi-
ment. In some poems, mostly in the poet's free-verse experi-
ments, end-rhyme is missing. The section entitled "Slabs from
a Sun-Down World" contains none. In the first section, "Out of
the Night," rhymes are numerous, but they are also very
regular:

Consider the Poet
(For Roland Carter)

Go back to earth and note how well
    Sweet grass will grow beneath your feet.
Touch it to see if grass will tell
    Temper in a different heat.

Go where the sympathetic rain
    Forgets to quench an underfire,
Rain drenched in and out again
    Lost in the wonderment of desire.

---

24. *Poetic Meter and Poetic Form*, p. 180.

> Go back to earth where many years
> Have dimmed his lettered stone;
> Bend low to give a poet poet's tears
> For each will claim you for her own.
>
> (p. 22)

For the contemporary reader, sounds such as these are unimpressive because they are too much alike. Only in the second stanza does one find anything resembling variety. The off-rhyme in "rain" and "again" is pleasing. The words "well" and "will," from the first two lines of stanza one, are brought together as "will tell" at the end of three, which also is pleasing.

One sees other evidence of the poet's experiments in *Harvest of Youth,* even though rhyme is seldom less perfect than that of "know" and "crow" (p. 14). There are off-rhymes such as "stove—shove" and "hearth—mirth" (p. 15). One can also find examples of light rhyme (matching a masculine ending with a feminine one), such as "man—Puritan" (p. 18). The poet frequently employs feminine or falling rhymes: "seven—Heaven" (p. 18), "yellow—fellow" (p. 19). He sometimes damages the poem by wrenching or warping syntax to force rhyme:

> Then I met with Youthful Sin
> And he threw wide his door;
> He bade me walk freely in
> And love him to the core.
>
> (p. 17)

In some instances, he chooses an inappropriate word (one which does not fit the tone of the poem) in order to secure sameness of sound:

> For the God that I had known
> I was a fool to love.
> When each day brought no return
> From his stale love thereof.
>
> (p. 18)

As an expression in itself, "love thereof" has archaic and Biblical connotations. And even though it is not suitable, it completes the syllable count and sounds like "love." Archaic forms occasionally become conspicuous as rhyme words:

> The winds are fairly whining
> Where Ann Rutledge sleeps;
> The pine trees are a-pining
> Where a tall man weeps.
> (p. 68)

A result of having to find a word that resembles "whining," the pun in line three destroys an otherwise serious poem. One finds examples of chiastic rhyme in the juvenilia, as brilliant and difficult as it is. The first stanza of "Sleep Spell," for example, begins with this: "Falls the rain, the rain is falling" (p. 69); the second stanza begins: "Whines the wind, the wind is whining." The young poet also uses internal rhyme. In "Carver Life" there are eight quatrains, and the third line of each rhymes internally: "If Love was late / I would not wait" (p. 71). As exercises in sonics, the early poems are not modern. Nor has there been much improvement in this respect throughout the poet's career.

What one ultimately arrives at in the way of an assessment of the juvenilia can be summarized by bringing together the references to Eliot, Cunningham, and Engle. The Twenties and Thirties saw American culture in rapid transition, and writers were abandoning the old ways—what Cunningham calls the "repetitive harmony of an old tradition." Stuart, however, was writing about what he knew—a place and a people where the old cultural ways were still apparently intact. And as Paul Engle aptly observes, the young poet chose "to keep the traditional ways" in writing as well. As much as anything else, this explains the problems in the juvenilia. The difficulty with Stuart's rhyme is that it belongs to the old way, as is the case with much of his diction. The difficulty with his sonnets is that they also belong to the old way. In *Harvest of Youth* and after, all of his experiments in "making the sonnet form usable" have been conducted by someone else at one time or another. When he came home from Vanderbilt University in 1932, he had decided more than ever that the old way was the right one. Since most of American culture was undergoing a much more rapid transition than Appalachia, there are obviously many implications in his decision that bear directly upon his becoming a regional writer.[25] As the poems in *Harvest of Youth* indicate, he was caught between two worlds, and although he would continue to flirt with the new one, throughout his career he would never abandon the old. In that respect, if for no other reason, the poems in the juvenilia proved to be remarkably successful.

---

25. Much too involved to be treated here, the topic of regionalism will be dealt with in Chapter 8.

4

The Poet As Craftsman:
A Will And a Way

Stuart's resolution to be himself after Vanderbilt must be viewed with considerable caution for the simple reason that he remained ambiguous about what he thought himself to be. He apparently had no delusions about *Harvest of Youth*. Moreover, he knew that it would take a more substantial book to make him a poet. But as disappointed as he might have been with his early experiments, he was confident enough to have some of the sonnets reprinted in *Man with a Bull-Tongue Plow*.[1] Further, the clearest evidence that he had confidence in *Harvest of Youth* lies in the fact that *Man with a Bull-Tongue Plow* consists of 703 sonnets, the form with which he experimented most diligently in his first collection. His progression as a craftsman begins with *Harvest of Youth* (cautious experiment), works through *Man with a Bull-Tongue Plow* (spontaneity), and climaxes in *Album of Destiny* (maturity and control).

In *Man with a Bull-Tongue Plow* the poet tends to move away from emphasis upon the iamb as an arithmetical norm from which to make controlled departures.[2] Continuing to

1. See Hargis Westerfield's Introduction in *Harvest of Youth* (Berea, Kentucky, 1964).
2. For a discussion of meter as arithmetical norm, see Yvor Winters, "The Audible Reading of Poetry," *The Function of Criticism* (Denver, 1957), p. 82. Winters writes, "Meter is the arithmetical norm, the purely theoretic structure of the line; rhythm is controlled departure from that norm."

count syllables, he explores ways of creating patterns of sounds and musical effects which derive from the thought and structure of the line. Accordingly, reiterations of various kinds set up recognizable sound patterns. He never completely abandons the iamb; the nature of the language will not allow it, at least not for very long.[3] Instead, he develops a system of parallels and phonic reiterations which remind one of Whitman, and for which Whitman appears to be the model. Devices like this do not necessarily exclude accentual patterns, but what seems strange is that Stuart, while using Whitman's prosodic techniques, would persist in writing sonnets, and in counting syllables. The result of what appears to be a strange admixture is that the style which he achieves in his rhythmic handling of language is peculiarly his own.

The poet's interest in sounds is an old one. He has always had his ear attuned to the noises around him. As early as his carnival days, he was listening discreetly:

> I heard different sounds from those made by the whippoorwills and katydids and of waters falling and crickets singing. . . . I heard voices all day long. I heard cries of anger and fits of laughter. Voices all day long and part of the night.

> (BDH, p. 116)

---

3. There are a number of considerations here, one of the most important of which is the placing of function words immediately before form classes for the sake of building syntactic units (for example: a horse, the man, that place, from them). In addition to the matter of syntax, and related to it, is the nature of stress in the English language. We front the stress (for example: fáther, rébel). This tendency is remarkably persistent, and is accounted for in Verner's Law. See Albert C. Baugh, *A History of the English Language* (New York, 1957), pp. 22 and 69. At least in part these are what constitute the explanation which Winters refers to in his "Audible Reading of Poetry." As he observes, "English verse is predominately iambic in structure" (p. 91). Because it is, he adds, "rhythm ceases to be rhythm, and becomes merely movement, whenever the norm itself is no longer discernible" (p. 94).

Often, while experimenting with sonorous effects, he plays
with them—apparently for sheer delight:

> The wind blows high tonight—the wind blows strong,
> The yellow leaves fall on the Sandy water,
> The leaves are grains of meal that sift among
> The naked boughs and the buff-colored fodder,
> The moon rides high—a grain of yellow dent,
> The oak trees rock—the yellow dent goes by,
> He smiles at silent fields in half-contempt—
> The wind and trees sing him a lullaby:
> "Tra-la—tra-la—tra-la—the moon is high,
> Tra-la—tra-la—tra-le—the moon is corn,
> O corn-moon, do you hear the hunter's horn?
> O corn-moon, do you hear the dead leaves sigh?
> Tra-la—tra-la—tra-le—tra-le—tra-li—
> Tra-le-tra-li—the moon is yellow corn."
>   (MWBTP, p. 185)

The lullaby is obviously a source of amusement, but some
of the rhythmical effects elsewhere in the poem deserve
attention.

Punctuation is the key to analysis of sound patterns. The
caesura (marked by the dash) in the first line is equivalent to a
line-end pause. The result is that the second half repeats the
grammatical pattern of the first and sets up or initiates
rhythms that control the poem. Grammatical structure is re-
peated in the first half of line five, on both sides of the caesura
in six, in the last half of eight, in the last half of nine, and in
the last half of fourteen. In addition to grammatical duplica-
tion, which is characterized by a change from subject-verb-
adjective to subject-verb-complement, words are repeated in
one place or another. "Moon" is substituted for "wind" in line
five, and the verb of being for the action verb in nine. Varia-
tions are thereby closely controlled. By placing the dash in the
middle of the line, the poet modulates the basic rhythms of the
poem. In the first line the second half echoes the thought of the
first, and in doing so receives both weaker stress and lower

pitch. As a result, stress tends to be weaker and pitch lower after the caesura in other lines, as in five and six, for example. Such deliberate modulation of sound presupposes the poem as voice, as "audible reading." One should never lose sight of the fact that the poem, for Jesse Stuart, exists somewhere beyond words. "Tra-la—tra-la—tra-la" has no meaning, and hardly sounds like the wind in the tops of trees. The most that one can say is that there is an exclusive rhythmic pattern—one which exists, in this case, apart from lexical meaning.

In other poems, the poet has come even closer to representing sounds which exist beyond rather than in words. Here, for instance, he tries to catch the cadence of a beating drum:

Dead leaves and damp—her bare feet touch the leaves.
The high winds blow—black pine trees wave and sigh.
The oak limbs crackle and a tree-top weaves
Black fingers patterned on the silver sky.
She waits—her lover comes—her brown-skin comes—
She knows he will come by a moon-lit stream—
Her steps are lighter than a far-off drum
Of rain against the leaves—she waits—she dreams—
"Tata-tatum—tata-tatum—tum—tum—
Tata-tatum—tata-tatum—tum—tum—"
Her lover comes—her brown-skin lover comes—
He proudly marches to the old war drum.
"Tata-tatum—tata-tatum—tum—tum—"
Her lover comes—her proud young lover comes.[4]

The caesura in the middle of each of the first two lines serves as sufficient stop or pause to build up a short and tight

---

4. MWBTP, p. 180. Stuart continues and improves upon this practice in *Album of Destiny* (New York, 1944). See, for example, the last sonnet in "Songs of the Silent Snow," in which the dripping rain becomes confused with the ticking of a clock (p. 172). Also see "A Winter Dirge for Rene Madden Crump," in which the rain becomes tears dripping onto the earth, mourning the death of a beautiful woman (p. 203).

rhythmic unit, which is released by running line three over into four. The tension is increased again in line five, relaxed in six and seven, and increased again in line five, relaxed in six and seven, and increased again in eight. The release comes again in twelve. The drum beat itself enhances the short and taut rhythmic unit at other places in the poem, and the caesura once again clearly marks its boundaries. The "tum," appearing at the end of lines, weakens in stress and lowers in pitch with characteristic modulation downward. In the meantime, there are clearly recognizable iambs. The recurrence of "her lover comes" characterizes the iambic pattern over which the rhythms of the poem are controlled. The result is a kind of counterpoint in which the iambs buck against the larger rhythmical unit and, in so doing, produce impressive results.

How much the poet emphasizes the dash in marking the caesura is indicated by his also placing dashes at the ends of lines. The pause there is the same as the one within the line, and the consequence is that emphasis is placed on movement, on stopping and starting, on punctuating a stream or continuum of sounds as voice or speech:

> She waits—her lover comes—her brown-skin comes—
> She knows he will come by a moon-lit stream—
> Her steps are lighter than a far-off drum
> Of rain against the leaves—she waits—she dreams—

Rhythm depends upon repetition, and in this case one should look beyond the beating of the drum. The two-syllable "brown-skin" replaces "lover" in line five: "She waits—her lover comes—her brown-skin comes—." In eight, the subject-verb sequence appears again: "Of rain against the leaves—she waits—she dreams—." What resembles an echo in eleven remains unchanged, except for the insertion of "brown-skin": "Her lover comes—her brown-skin lover comes—." Fourteen is similar. The adjectives are added: "Her lover comes—her proud young lover comes." These lines indicate something of the effectiveness of the poet's use of repetition in building rhythmic patterns. According to C. Alfonso Smith,

In prose, a word or group of words is repeated for emphasis; where in verse, repetition is chiefly employed not for emphasis (compare the use of the refrain), but for melody of rhythm, for continuousness or sonorousness of effect, for unity of impression, for banding lines or stanzas, and for purposes of suggestiveness.[5]

Smith, of course, is accurate only in part. In verse, repetition may be employed for the sake of emphasis, as much of this chapter demonstrates. Unfortunately, though, one has no choice but to talk in generalities when the subject is rhythm. As Harvey Gross says in the Introduction to his collection of essays on prosody, the matter is "too tenuous and variable for exact analysis."[6]

Stuart relies more heavily upon alliteration and assonance in *Man with a Bull-Tongue Plow*, but his foremost prosodic principles are those of reiterating and paralleling. He never abandons the sonnet. The following lines contain an example of the poet's alliterations and reiterations:

Sweet summer here with bud and bloom and breeze
And tall bronze men beneath wind-laps of grain—
Sweet summer here with wind among the trees,
With wind among the flowers and honey bees—
Among the flowers—beneath the stars above—
The silver wind plays with the stars above,
With flowers and moonlight on the leafy trees—
Plays with the ferns and trees and clouds above
And summer fields that I have learned to love.
(MWBTP, p. 7)

Assessed for their sonic value, rhymes are as regular as usual, and the alliterating *b* and *s* sounds are obvious. Apparently, the initial "Sweet summer" is repeated in line three in order to establish mellowness of tone. The major controlling device

---

5. *Repetition and Parallelism in English Verse* (New York, 1894), p. 9.
6. *The Structure of Verse: Modern Essays on Prosody* (Greenwich, Connecticut, 1966), p. 13.

is the preposition: "with bud and bloom and breeze," "With wind among the flowers," "with the stars above," "With flowers and moonlight," "with the ferns and trees and clouds," "beneath wind-laps of grain," "beneath the stars above," "among the trees," "among the flowers and honey bees," and "Among the flowers." Granted, there are other structures, but the prepositional phrase has its own characteristic intonation contour—which goes far in shaping the rhythmic patterns of the above lines.[7]

Reiterations are not usually as scattered as those above, but rather are often remarkably systematic. Numerous sonnets in *Man with a Bull-Tongue Plow* contain examples of anaphora. These lines—from many which the poet wrote about his father—are typical:

> And now his love is wind among the corn;
> His love is whispering, talking, green corn blades.
> His love is cornfields when the summer fades,
> Oak leaves to red and fodder blades to brown.
> His love is autumn raining dead leaves down
> And going out on autumn morns to salt the stock.
> He loves his mules and whispering corn at night—
> Buff-colored corn in full autumn moonlight. (p. 28)

The recurrence of "His love" is either different enough or broken enough in lines one, four, six, and eight to make it effective, even though the poetry is prosaic and poor. Repetitions other than the initial ones are also important. Occurring throughout, "corn" is a notable example.

Especially marked by anaphora in *Man with a Bull-Tongue Plow* are those sonnets in which Stuart constructs his catalogues. As many as ten of fourteen lines sometimes begin with the same expression. This one from the farewell sequence is typical:

---

7. Paralleling is grammatical and consists of placing constructions alongside each other. Reiterating is merely the repeating of any unit of structure; the units need not be (but may be) placed side by side.

Farewell to Springtime in Kentucky hills;
Farewell to dogwood blossoms and percoon;
To blood-root in the wind and daffodils
To wild plum blossoms and white April moon.
Farewell to walnut trees beside the river;
Farewell to April's sky-blue singing brooks;
Farewell to young thin April leaves that quiver;
Farewell to white clouds mirrored in the brooks.
Farewell to Spring wheat waving in the wind
And rank potatoes bursting from the ground;
Farewell to shower-clouds watery-thinned
And to the far-off cow bell's lonely sound.
Farewell to April and bright bull-tongue plows;
Farewell to green pastures and spotted cows.

(p. 340)

Here the initial duplications and the line-end punctuation indicate rather definitely that the line is the rhythmic unit, and that it is also the unit of sense. The sentence and the line correspond, and even where they do not, as in two and three, they are punctuated as though they did. Although they are not punctuated at the end, lines nine and eleven are marked by syntactic breaks before the subordinate conjunction which begins the next line. Hence, the intonation contour is completed at the end.

That the rhymes are intended to be more than sonic or acoustic should be evident. Coming at the end of the sentence and the line, they are rhetorically, visually, rhythmically, and semantically significant. All of the end-rhymes, except two, are nouns, although each appears in a quite different context. As linguistic symbols placed in emphatic positions, they exercise control over semantic environment. They are emblematic and extremely complementary to cataloguing and paralleling. Pictorially, they aid in arranging or focusing visual details into larger groups. As far as logic is concerned, "hills," at the end of line one, is not only in the strongest position in the line, but in the entire poem. Inductively, it would have to come last. Everything named or asserted points back to "in Kentucky hills." Finally, an "April moon" (line four) which shines on "daffodils" and "percoon" (lines three and two) which are found in "Kentucky hills" (line one) is not just any moon. It gets its meaning from its context.

Sometimes in *Man with a Bull-Tongue Plow* Stuart duplicates the entire line:

> I do not know if these are things they wanted.
> I do not care if these are things they wanted. (p. 282)

Lines five and seven, and thirteen and fourteen, contain similar examples within the same sonnet. Some of the poems which rely heavily upon recurrence of the whole line are effectively done. The following is typical:

> When he marched on the poppy fields of Flanders,
> When he marched on the shell-torn land of France,
> Two ghosts, tall ghosts, kept step with him in
>   Flanders,
> Two ghosts, tall ghosts, kept step with him in France.
> One on each side they marched by him in Flanders,
> Went marching, marching, marching endlessly.
> One on each side, they saw him laid in Flanders,
> They marched away together there—those three;
> And one tall ghost was dressed in Northern blue,
> And one tall ghost was dressed in Southern gray,
> Beside a youth in khaki they went marching,
> Beneath the stars and stripes they marched away.
> Down through all times these three go marching,
>   marching,
> Go marching, marching, marching endlessly. (p. 302)

The rhythms of such a poem are extremely pleasing, and the pleasure derives from making line two so much like one, and ten so much like nine. In a longer poem, the poet can reproduce the same line over and over again. Or he can repeat an entire stanza, as is often done in the case of the refrain.[8] Be-

---

8. Whitman often does it. See "By Blue Ontario's Shore," *Complete Poetry and Prose* (New York, 1948), I, 307. In the same source, see "When Lilacs Last in the Dooryard Bloom'd," p. 298.

cause of the limitations of the sonnet Stuart reiterates different lines and often places them back to back. Exemplified in the "marching" sonnet above, such an arrangement indicates the extent to which the line, by the time of *Man with a Bull-Tongue Plow,* was becoming both the rhythmic unit and the unit of sense. Each line is either a sentence or a major syntactic unit quite capable of standing alone rhythmically.

One can find effective examples of line-medial reiteration in *Man with a Bull-Tongue Plow*:

> I see the blood of autumn in the wind,
> The wine-red blood of apple-tree and peach;
> The yellow blood of poplar tree and beech;
> I see the blood of autumn drifting in
> The fence rows and the stools of green briar
>   thickets;   (p. 217)

The entire poem from which these lines were taken depends heavily upon anaphora. Still, "blood" appears in exactly the same spot in the first four. After that the word is missing for three lines. Then it occurs five times within four, during which it is interchanged with "mood." Using the often restated "blood," in line nine the poet sets up a full-line pattern. Lines eleven and fifteen, in which he substitutes "mood" for "blood," follow the pattern established in nine:

> O blood of autumn, you are in my blood—
> Red shoe-make blood is in my dead-leaf veins;
> O mood of autumn, you are in my mood;
> Only, your red of shoe-make blood remains
> And mine does not—I am a naked tree—
> The winds have blown—my autumn is on me.
> (O mood of autumn, you are in my mood!)
>   (p. 217)

Line-final patterns are not frequently found in *Man with a Bull-Tongue Plow.* The sonnets contain close and exacting rhymes which have their own impact. But even though end-rhyme is usually present, one occasionally encounters something like this:

> The poplar leaves drift in a windy flood,
> From their tall tops drift slowly to the ground.
>
> (p. 183)

The word "drift" is restated, and is in both cases followed by a prepositional phrase.

The object here is not to account for all of Stuart's duplicating devices; they are far too numerous for that. The most that can be hoped for is that those which are consistently and effectively used (and which are readily explicable) can be identified and illustrated in one way or another. In addition to the usual repetitions—the single word within the line, the line, line-initial patterns, line-medial patterns, and line-final patterns—there are other significant techniques which Stuart employs in *Man with a Bull-Tongue Plow* in order to produce and control rhythms. One of these is what Gay Wilson Allen refers to as grammatical rhythm,[9] which simply consists of building rhythmic effects through repeating a particular part of speech (as in semantic rhyme) or grammatical construction:

> Sweet summer here with wind among the trees,
> With wind among the flowers and honey bees—
> Among the flowers—beneath the stars above—
>
> (p. 7)

The preposition is the part of speech which sets up and progresses rhythmic control: "with wind among the trees, / With wind among the flowers." One tends to insert "with wind" in the third line, before "Among the flowers," and before "beneath the stars." Recurring in this way, the preposition is very successful in building and maintaining the rhythmic structure of the poem. Equally interesting are these lines from a sonnet about Mae Marberry, a flower picker:

9. For a discussion of this and other devices, see *Walt Whitman Handbook* (New York, 1946), pp. 408-409.

> A slender child, she gathers flowers today,
> She gathers blue sweet-williams from the woods
> Where trees are still unleafed and woods are gray.
> She gathers wild-flowers from these solitudes,
> Wind-flowers and sweet-williams while she may.
>
> (p. 24)

The subject-verb-object sequence is duplicated as a unit, but the noun in the position of the object carries over into line four and continues the rhythms: "she gathers flowers," "She gathers blue sweet-williams," "She gathers wild-flowers," "Wind-flowers and sweet-williams." the objects alone are these: "flowers," "sweet-williams," "wild-flowers," "Wind-flowers," and "sweet-williams." The subject-verb-object pattern itself is rhythmic even when repeated as it is here. Any one of the three—subject, verb, or object—may continue to carry the rhythms once the trend has been established.

Another such device which Stuart counts on in *Man with a Bull-Tongue Plow* is that of logical rhyme or rhythm, which consists of naming things that are in their logical places, or things that are in the process of doing what they logically do:

> Do you hear creaking of the big ox cart
> Over the Kentucky wilderness road?
> Ah, don't your hear the creaking heavy load
> And cattle panting under the heavy load?
>
> (p. 303)

In these lines he does a number of unusual things, including repeating "heavy load" at the end of the line. One would expect a heavy ox cart to creak, and he would expect the oxen pulling the cart to pant. They are evidence that the load is heavy; otherwise they would not be doing what they logically do. The poet's lists and catalogues also lend themselves to the use of grammatical rhyme:

> Farewell to birds a-roosting in the fodder;
> Farewell to naked hills with white-rock seams,

To black leaves drifting on the slushy water;[10]

Birds normally roost, and leaves drift on water. Such a practice could prove hampering if it were tightened up so that a logical statement occurred in each line. Other kinds of recurrence are numerous. Anaphora is obvious, and end-rhyme is apparent. The verbals positioned in the middle of lines one and three result in heavy reiteration at the beginning, in the middle, and at the end.

He also utilizes cognates for rhythmic effect:

> And I can sing my lays like singing corn,
> And flute them like a fluting gray corn-bird;
>
> (p. 3)

In line one the adjective "singing" is anticipated by the verb "sing," which precedes it. In two, the adjective "fluting" is cognate to the verb preceding it. That he chooses to derive his words in the same way, and that he sets the results at about the same position in their relationship to the preceding verb, aids in rhythmic control of the line, and ultimately in control of the entire poem. A similar passage appears much later, in the Plum Grove section:

> To hell with singers' sentimental songs,
> Let them go sing for men where they belong.
> Give us a singer that will sing for us—
> The truth of us—then listen to his song
> For we must sleep—and our sleep shall be long!
>
> (p. 284)

Line one contains "singers' ... songs." Two contains "sing," and three contains both "singer" and "sing." Line four ends with "song." In addition to repeating derivatives in this way, Stuart also takes a simple word like "corn" and compounds it into several forms such as "corn rows," "corn blades," "cornfields," and "corn shocks":

---

10. P. 189. The same vowel is repeated. Note, however, the consonance in "fodder" and "water." Stuart's dialect does not distinguish between the voiced d and the voiceless t.

> And now his love is wind among the corn;
> His love is whispering, talking green corn blades.
> His love is cornfields when the summer fades,
>
> (p. 28)

The compounds here are not derived in the sense that "sings" and "singer," found in the preceding lines, come from the verb meaning "to sing." Both processes, all the same, have to do with forming words, with units of sound to be repeated, and in that respect serve the same purpose rhythmically.

To progress from an investigation of reiterating in *Man with a Bull-Tongue Plow* to one of paralleling in *Album of Destiny* is not to experience a major break in the development of Jesse Stuart's prosodic techniques. *Album of Destiny* contains all of the techniques found in the earlier book, but here emphases change. For one, the numerous caesuras are no longer marked by the dash. The great number of dashes found throughout *Man with a Bull-Tongue Plow* all but disappear. The few which remain exist primarily to indicate a break or change in voice—to interrupt, momentarily, what is otherwise a series of closely paralleled lines:

> I shall not miss our neighbors and our mules;
> I shall not miss our cattle, fields and trees;
> I shall not miss my home, my folks, farm tools—
> While battering steel, I shall not think of these.
>
> (AD, p. 44)

The last line in the series has the impact of a summary or conclusion. It is prolonged by inserting the dash, and by following the dash with "While battering steel." This throws the expression which balances those in preceding lines to the very end.

In *Album of Destiny* the dashes appear for two major reasons. The first is that Stuart increasingly relies on ellipsis marks to indicate a break or change which results momentarily in suspending the general rhythmical pattern:

> I shall return to feel Kentucky heat
> And April showers that quickly cool the air,
> Return to tramp my hills on tireless feet . . .
> I wish to God tonight that I were there!   (p. 134)

The shift is made obvious by marking it in this way. In some cases such a practice not only indicates a shift but also sets off an emphatic assertion:

> Mace Bushman told me when he married me
> He'd take me far away from whistle screams,
> Said he would take me where we would be free
> In his Kentucky . . . . Such an idle dream!
> To hear the Pittsburgh whistles scream again
> Would fill me, thrill me . . . music in my ears!
> To think of Pittsburgh's noisy streets again,
> And clouds of smoke, my eyes filled up with tears.
> (p. 138)

In these lines Bettie Coyle Bushman is both telling her story and commenting upon it. The ellipsis marks are used to separate the story from the commentary. A second reason for the near-disappearance of the dash is that the poet turns away from breaking the line. More than in previous work, the line becomes the unit of structure and the unit of thought in *Album of Destiny*. Occasionally, he does not bother with appropriate end-punctuation, but simply uses commas:

> I did not plan this winter for the dead,
> I did not make this rain and send the snow,
> I did not send each to his narrow bed
> To lie forever with the dirt below;[11]

Continuing to organize his sonnets by quatrain, he sometimes

---

11. P. 167. Furthermore, composing by line often leads to the poet's inserting commas where they do not belong:
> This tough-shelled whiteoak sprout with emerald bud
> That rots into the earth above his face,
> Will grow from dust of him and drink his blood
> And blossom prettily in wind-blue space. (p. 236)

punctuates the second and fourth lines with other than commas, even though each one contains a complete sentence:

> Tonight we have forgotten slopes we've plowed,
> We have forgotten corn our hands have wrought;
> We have forgotten sun and rain and cloud,
> We have forgotten battles we have fought. (p. 55)

Another characteristic arrangement within the quatrain is that of making the sentence and the quatrain correspond. The first line often makes an assertion, and each of the next three contains a subordinate structure which balances the one in the first. In the following example each line except the last is marked off by a comma:

> And I remember how we vowed by waters,
> And how we pledged eternal troths of love,
> And how the ferns did kiss the foaming waters,
> And what it was to live the spring of love.[12]

There are also instances of making the line and the sentence correspond in which the poet overruns the end of the quatrain for the sake of paralleling four lines and then releases the rhythms in the fifth:

> We pluck the sweet wild purple thistle blossom,
> We love the smell of heated pasture grass,
> We love the sun that wilts the shoe-string vines,
> We love the summer dome of high blue grass
> Where sun rays drip the color of old wine. (p. 76)

Again, the line is the unit of structure and the unit of thought. The pattern of rhythms is broken or released by continuing the thought of the fourth line into the fifth.

Such treatment of the line as is illustrated in the above passages poses numerous interesting possibilities. In the first place, the impact of Whitman on Jesse Stuart becomes even more obvious in *Album of Destiny,* and the foremost technique

---

12. P. 125. The emphatic form of the verb in the middle of the third line may be intended, but probably not. It appears to be padding.

is that of the parallel. The parallel, according to Gay Wilson Allen, arises from the same psychological impulse as does the catalogue, and achieves the same general effects of "poetic identification."[13] Hence, it is no accident that the line becomes the unit of rhythm and the unit of thought. Stuart's need to be a pioneer, to be an individual, would not allow him to settle for traditional prosodic techniques alone. There is no way of knowing how much he relied on Whitman. The King James Version of the Bible could have influenced him just as much. In Hebrew poetry, the line, contends Allen, was also the unit, "and the second line balanced the first, completing or supplementing its meaning."[14] A further possibility is found in primitive poetry. As Allen says, parallelism is apparently found in most primitive poetry, and many translations of Indian songs and chants contain parallels.[15] In his work, from *Harvest of Youth* to the present, Jesse Stuart has never abandoned his concern for the primitive. W-Hollow, in both his poetry and his fiction, is a primitive place where man is "brother to the tree."[16] Mary Washington Clarke's survey of folklore is in effect an index to his knowledge of primitivism.[17] Also, his early preoccupation with the ballad, which relies for much of its effectiveness upon repetends and refrains, doubtless had considerable influence on his adopting the parallel. Finally, in the larger context of his trying to lift his W-Hollow milieu to literature, such a practice appears to be a natural thing. W-Hollow people are close to the soil, possess limited vocabularies, count heavily on memory, and cultivate economy of language which lends itself well to balance and antithesis.

---

13. *Walt Whitman Handbook*, p. 399.
14. *Ibid.*, p. 389.
15. *American Prosody* (New York, 1966), p. 174.
16. Such references are actually quite numerous. See *Album of Destiny*, p. 73.
17. The survey referred to here is *Jesse Stuart's Kentucky* (New York, 1968). Clarke has also published papers on folklore in the writings of Stuart.

The technique consists of repeating grammatical constructions, and to repeat the construction is to repeat the rhythms. The main principle involved is that of controlling thoughts—balancing them alongside each other. For Whitman, the unit of sense was the measure of the line,[18] and that this is a major concern of Stuart's has already been demonstrated. The line makes an independent statement, and is often either a complete or elliptical sentence. Repeating the idea, with some variation, produces the effect of chanting, and is therefore rhapsodic. Whitman used the construction to bind lines together and thereby form units similar to the stanza in conventional versification.[19] The W-Hollow poet, by contrast, uses the sonnet form to shape externally. He employs parallel construction to shape from within, constantly pushing outward toward the external form. This becomes his "measure of freedom" in bucking against traditional form, and in doing so allows him the individuality which he has persistently stressed as more important to the poet than to any other person.[20] Coleridge says that organic form shapes as it develops itself "from within, and the fullness of its development is one and the same with the perfection of its outward form. Such as the life is, such is the form."[21] In Coleridge's sense, Stuart can never be called an organic poet, even though he pushes toward organicism and settles for a compromise—a maximum of shaping from within toward a minimum of form from with-

---

18. *Walt Whitman Handbook*, p. 393.
19. *Ibid.*, p. 397.
20. "Meeting Mr. New England, America's Greatest Poet," *Education Forum* 23 (1959), 291-292. In this essay Stuart reports a discussion which took place between Frost and himself about the poet as an individual. He writes, "The first question Robert Frost asked me was what I thought of schools of poetry. I was slow to tell him what I actually thought, but he wasn't very slow about telling me what he thought. He disagreed with all of them." The W-Hollow poet agreed with Frost, and was very happy when Frost told him, "He thought every poet should be an individualist."
21. *Essays and Lectures on Shakespeare and Some Other Old Poets and Dramatists* (London, n.d.), pp. 46-47.

out.[22] This does not, it seems, completely exclude him from believing, as Whitman did, that a poetic experience "will find its own natural rhythm in the act of expression."[23]

In the envelope of thought parallelism, writes Allen, "the initial line states an idea or a proposition, succeeding lines state parallel thoughts regarding the first line, and the final line states a concluding thought."[24] Stuart's attempts, because of the size of the sonnet form, are characterized by a limited number of lines—usually two or three. In *Album of Destiny* he never develops the envelope as Whitman did, for example, in "Joy, Shipmate, Joy."[25] All the same, he does employ similar techniques.

He uses synthetic or constructive parallelism[26] in which the second line (and sometimes others) supplements or completes the first:

> Better to give companionship to man
> Than take your strong proud body back to earth;
> (p. 111)

He also makes use of a synonymous form, in which the second line enforces the thought of the first by reproducing and echoing it, but with variation:

> Descend upon us, night of green spring love!
> Descend upon us, O, Great Night of love.
> (p. 102)

He cultivates antithesis, in which the last line denies or contrasts what comes before it:

> There is no need to speak for death of flowers,

22. There is always a question of how minimal the sonnet is as external form. However, it should be kept in mind that the sonnet for Stuart is a field to be filled, and that the poet's task consists of filling it. The field itself is merely accepted.
23. *Walt Whitman Handbook*, p. 410.
24. *American Prosody*, p. 225.
25. *Complete Poetry and Prose*, I, 428.
26. See Allen's *Walt Whitman Handbook*, pp. 389-392, for a discussion of parallelism.

> There is no need to speak for butterflies
> That used to flit and while away the hours
> On dotted silken wings beneath blue skies.
> But there is need to speak for you, my love;
>
> (p. 123)

He frequently employs climax, in which the last line takes up words from the first and completes the statement which began there:

> I go into the fields before the dawn.
> I go into the fields to husk my corn.
>
> (p. 113)

Success here obviously depends on whether the last line completes a statement or simply adds one. A paraphrase looks like this: Before dawn I go into the fields to husk my corn. There is little doubt, however, about the success of these lines:

> Come on, my brothers, unafraid of hell,
> Come on and meet each dark slump on the wind;
>
> (p. 215)

The poet's accomplishment in using parallels does not depend entirely upon his hewing to the four kinds illustrated here. What he does best may be conceived of as departures from and variations upon them. He is always in the position of having to consider the demands of the sonnet as form. With such restrictions in mind, he looks for and finds ways of gliding on and off balance, of springing loose from it once a rhythmic pattern has lost its effectiveness and threatens to become monotonous. He frequently makes a simple synonymous statement:

> I want to sleep where kindred dust reposes,
> I want the land they own to sleep upon.
>
> (p. 104)

Sometimes he confuses the synonymous and synthetic forms:

> She will be gayer than swift dashing water,

Gayer than April wind in spring-bloomed phlox.
(p. 105)

The poet often springs the end of the second line loose in a synonymous statement, and lets the next two or three lines make the statement that repeats or echoes the one in the first:

> Peace comes to me tonight among these hills;
> Peace comes with darkness and the sullen skies,
> With calling of the valley whippoorwills
> And light in velvet darkness of fireflies. (p. 64)

The success of a structure like this depends upon much more than the similarity of the first two lines. Part of the impact is carried over into the third line, and largely through the preposition. The "And" at the beginning of the fourth replaces the "With" at the beginning of the third. The result is that the first two lines begin synonymously, and the next two pick up some part of them, forming what appears to be another parallel. The statement in the last two lines becomes a variation upon the one in the first two. Rhythmically, the result is pleasing because something of the first is retained, but also because something new is added. There is both similarity and difference, likeness and unlikeness.

In *Album of Destiny* Stuart's practice of composing by line, and then grouping the lines into quatrains, has considerable influence on what he does with parallels. The quatrain and the balanced idea seem to go together or to correspond, and there are various kinds of arrangements within any one quatrain:

> Over the wastelands, to my neck in briars,
> Over the hollows and their swollen creeks,
> And through white streaks of light from stars'
>   white fires,
> I run on iron legs with wind that speaks!
(p. 60)

The lines that are similar build up to an emphatic and climactic statement, which is held until the end, and which does not parallel the other lines at all. The result is a kind of dramatic or rhetorical emphasis that proves successful. The alternative to structuring in this way is to place the emphatic statement first and let the balanced lines follow and fall away from it:

> Ettie will be beloved by Sammie Raines
> As long as beats this mountain heart of mine,
> As long as living blood flows through these veins
> And winds disturb the needles of the pine. (p. 205)

The difference may be little more than that which exists between a periodic and a loose sentence, but that does not make it any less striking.

Other arrangements of the parallel within the quatrain are equally impressive:

> Beat down on us, you welcome summer rain!
> Beat down on roots of corn you failed to feed
> In months of drouth that shriveled all our grain!
> Beat on our dying corn, our growing weed! (p. 85)

The second line is continued into the third, and the fourth resembles the first two. By extending the second, running it into the third, the pattern is broken and picked up again in the fourth, giving it an emphatic edge that would otherwise be missing. A similar effect may be created by making the first three lines alike and running the third over into the fourth:

> Too long a man must sleep where he is lain,
> Too long to sleep beneath a blinded moon,
> Too long beneath the spears of stabbing rain
> That penetrate the walls of his cocoon.
>
> (p. 195)

The fourth line is an extension of the third. It completes the statement and glides off the pattern which characterizes the first three. The two lines which resemble each other may exist in the middle of the quatrain:

> Down in this hollow's deep dark solitude

Where sun rays filter through the wind-swayed trees,
Where jarflies churr and snakes crawl through
  the wood,
I pillow myself on the grass with ease. (p. 235)

In a case like this, the third and fourth lines appear to be a way of postponing the closing statement in order to gain or build dramatic and rhetorical emphasis.

The parallels in the quatrains found in *Album of Destiny* are of various kinds and degrees. They may be relatively relaxed:

I told the wine-green April life was here,
That swift bright April life among our men,
A swift blood season of the fleeting year,
A glorious season not to come again! (p. 61)

Or they may be relatively intense:

Roll over, clouds, like ledges of thick stones!
Roll over me, dark clouds—roll over fast!
Roll over me tonight—I am alone;
Far in these windy woods I am alone! (p. 175)

They may exist in pairs of lines, with the second couple making a statement which is synonymous with the one in the first:

She should have known her body could not last
The stronger wine, the dance, the midnight hour;
She should have known that she could live too fast
And rush the season for her fragile power. (p. 196)

Lines which are alike sometimes overrun the limits of the quatrain:

Come Kathaleen, for soon we two shall lie
Under the winds that blow and feet that run;
Under the dirt we furrow in today;
Under the weeds we strike down with our hoes;
Under the dead-leaf rich Kentucky clay;
Under the wordless songs that the wind blows.
                    (p. 31)

Here they are subordinate clauses, but they may just as well
be coordinate:

> Lull, beetle, lull, white frost is near at hand,
> And white clouds shimmer through the heaven's blue,
> And water flows in meadow streams cold-blue,
> And yellow leaves drift on the sawbriar land. (p. 124)

It would be misleading to conclude this discussion with hav-
ing presented Stuart's parallels as though they existed in iso-
lation. These parallels do not consist merely in making one
structure fit one quatrain which just happens to appear in one
sonnet. Instead, balanced ideas exist as integral parts of the
whole poem. They may be, and often are, numerous, as in
these lines:

> Great summer Sun of Heaven, shine upon us!
> Throw golden rays, great Sun, on our bronze shoulders!
> We're grateful, Sun, for golden rays upon us,
> And knotted body muscles hard as boulders!
> We're grateful, Sun, for life, for earth, for bread.
> We're grateful, Sun, for brother-trees, for skies,
> For land to give us birth and hold our dead;
> We're grateful for the white rain in our eyes,
> We're grateful for the sting of blowing wind.
> We're grateful for our march toward the sun,
> Marching in the strong clay temples we are in,
> Marching, marching, marching to the sun;
> Marching in love with life and unafraid;
> Youth strong American with dreams ahead! (p. 73)

In many ways the above, in which John Sutton addresses his
wife Kathaleen, affords a fitting summary of the preceding
discussion. All lines of the sonnet are end-stopped, and com-
position is obviously by line. The first four are grouped into a
quatrain, although the next break is not as clear as the first
one. Rhyme is semantic and rhetorical, not merely acoustic.
Repetitions and parallels are plentiful—perhaps too much

so.[27] Granting, however, that the poem may be overwritten, one nevertheless can see the essence of the poet's mature work in it. The iambs are frequently strong, as they are in line seven. The lines of the sonnet (except one through four and eleven, with feminine endings) contain ten syllables each, and the form itself probably goes back as far as the first half of the thirteenth century.[28] The Whitmanesque or free-verse prosodic techniques are imposed upon what is otherwise traditional versification,[29] leaving little doubt that Stuart is a craftsman. The old mystique of the untutored singer cannot account for the craftsmanship in *Album of Destiny*. For a convincing explanation, one must go back to *Beyond Dark Hills*, Stuart's early autobiography. Here he writes: "I wanted to be different, not for the sake of being different but being different for something" (p. 229). The craftsmanship in *Album of Destiny* is his being different "for something." It is his way of trying to be both a poet and a self, for the poet, as Jesse Stuart knows, is ultimately a man.

---

27. Ruel Foster contends that the success of *Man with a Bull-Tongue Plow* is largely due to the spontaneity with which Stuart writes about his "bronze men of the earth." He likewise contends that too much form—too much striving to be a craftsman—is the major reason behind the poet's declining reputation after *Album of Destiny*. See *Jesse Stuart* (New York, 1968), p. 67.

28. See Patrick Cruttwell, *The English Sonnet* (London, 1966), p. 6. He writes that the inventor of the sonnet form appears to have been a poet at the court of Emperor Frederick II in Sicily. Frederick died in 1250.

29. All of the techniques used by the W-Hollow poet can be found in the work of practitioners of traditional versification. The contention here is that the practices in *Album of Destiny* have their origin in the experiments found in *Harvest of Youth*, and that Stuart's discovery of Whitman gave an added impetus toward the direction which he finally took. Rhyme, of course, is a notable exception. Whitman's poetry is for the most part stithic; Stuart's is strophic. It requires no great leap of the imagination, however, for a writer of strophes to identify semantic rhyme with Whitman's prosodic devices.

5

The Later Poems:
A Tree in The Wind

Album of Destiny (1944) marks the height of Jesse Stuart's career as poet, but certainly not as a writer. As a matter of necessity, the disappointment which came as a result of that collection's poor reception set him to reassessing his successes and failures. Having launched his poetry writing career in *Man with a Bull-Tongue Plow* (1934), he viewed *Album of Destiny* as an opportunity to establish himself—to gain a firm foothold in a growing American poetry. Such was the dream; the realities proved to be quite different.

After *Album of Destiny* one sees only a falling off, accompanied by what takes shape as a desperate search for a new beginning. There is a recognizable submission to the existence of open form, and a growing consciousness of what has come to be called the New Criticism (one of the directions taken by formalist criticism, which has its foundations in Aristotelian principles of art). More noticeable, and equally as important, is the poet's stubborn determination not to participate in either. Considering that both were gaining in popularity during the time in which *Album of Destiny* was being written, there is little wonder that Stuart is openly hostile toward them. His collection was dated and did not have a chance, even before it went to the publisher. Knowing that, he refused to change, even if he could have, although he had labored long and carefully for success. Ever conscious of his position and knowing well that he is out of the main stream, he waits and occasionally casts an aspersion:

> I have remained true to my beliefs, published or not. To hell with the publishing. I've had 1908 poems published—more to be published. It's true—but there are few markets that I would even send to. What is currently poetry—so-called—really isn't poetry. Time will show.[1]

Hopeful that the clock will be turned back, or that American experience will be shaped in new but meaningful forms, he persists in using the old ones until such a time actually arrives. In the meantime, he remains sensitive to trends in criticism:

> It is a tragic fate young Americans followed; older Americans switched to follow the New Criticism. Today, Dr. Harold Richardson, who hates the New Criticism with a passion, says it's cracking at the seams and going out. But it has left destruction in its wake. Such great American writers as Mark Twain and Thomas Wolfe were ruled out.[2]

In conversations and correspondence, Stuart frequently returns to what he wrote before World War II, when he was known primarily for his poetry. He reminisces enthusiastically about those days, and one soon senses that he continues to have pride in being a poet: "In earlier days, sometimes on a poetic binge, I'd write all night. A poem had to have form, choice words—poetic words. It had to have beauty and it had to say something."[3] The four requisites are important because they define the poet's concept of a poem, insofar as it can be defined. The last (the idea that a poem has to say something) is especially interesting because of his refusal to cut a poem loose from its history, and even more so because he also refuses

1. Letter to the writer, September 14, 1969.
2. Letter to the writer, September 12, 1969.
3. Letter to the writer, August 26, 1969.

to divorce the poem and its history from experience in the real
world. He documents a poem in much the same way that he
documents people. Its place is written into the Stuart canon.
Recently, he has resorted to publishing the history along with
the poem. "Love Song After Forty," one of a growing number of
such instances, published in *Hold April*, has been reprinted,
accompanied by a history of it, in *South*.[4] In a letter dated
September 9, 1969, he writes: "I am sending you eight poems
from *Album of Destiny* with histories behind them." In an ear-
lier letter, dated August 26, 1969, he sent seven poems and
their histories, saying that they had been accepted for an-
thologizing. The histories are strictly factual. A matter of
record-keeping, they almost always begin like this:

> On a stormy night in late summer 1943, I sat on our front
> porch until long after midnight while rain poured from
> low black skies. Lightning flashed around me, and thun-
> der rumbled loud enough to shake the earth. I was in a
> terrific mood. I wrote a poem, 160 lines, for our daughter.
> "Poem for My Daughter" was later published in *Com-
> monweal*.[5]

The practice seems eccentric, but Stuart compares his rela-
tionship to the poem with that of a doctor to his patient: "I
have found that I have written the body. A poem to me is a
body. Aristotle got it from his father, who was a doctor of
medicine."[6] As a body, the poem warrants its own record and,
as the poet would have us believe, a place in his chronicle. A
record of a people and their ideas, the chronicle encompasses a
substantially long period of time. Beginning with the earliest
settlers in the area, it continues into the present. The task of
writing a single region into the literature of the nation is
large, requiring a prophet in robes who conscientiously takes
upon himself the job of interpreting events. One should not,
therefore, be astounded by Jesse Stuart's reluctance to ac-

---

4. *See South* 3 (Fall 1970), 3-8.
5. Included in a letter to the writer, August 26, 1969.
6. Interview, taped at W-Hollow, May 31, 1971.

knowledge that poetry is well and healthy, or that it honestly reflects the national experience.

Refusing to adjust, and maintaining himself in a poet's exile, he concentrates on fiction, the output of which has increased in proportion to the decrease in poetry. In the ten years between *Man with a Bull-Tongue Plow* and *Album of Destiny*, he published two collections of stories, two novels, and a prose autobiography. Since that time, he has published two thin volumes of verse, consisting of a total of 147 poems, approximately one-eighth of the number in the two previous collections. During the same time, he has averaged a volume of prose each year, most of which is fiction. Since *Hold April* (1962), single poems and an occasional group have been printed in journals and magazines, but such occurrences are sparse. Presently, the poet has two unpublished manuscripts of poems in his possession— "Songs of a Mountain Plowman," written around 1931-1932, and "Birdland's Golden Age," which is still being added to.[7]

In *Kentucky Is My Land* (1952), one finds nothing in the way of a unifying device—certainly nothing approaching the previously used change of seasons or the metaphor of the photograph album. Instead, the poems appear in miscellaneous groups and are uneven in quality. The most one can say for them is that they seem to register the poet's moods and experiences in different situations and at different times. This is evident everywhere, and especially in the section entitled "Great Lakes Naval Training Station." One sees no advancement in prosodic technique beyond that achieved in *Album of Destiny*. What the reader does see, and probably welcomes, is a kind of gentle resignation or loosening up—less straining to become accepted—leading to a definite proclivity for prose, indicated by the two long prose poems which begin and end the collection. Considered together, loosening up of form and cultivation of the prose poem prepare the poet to write some of his finest lyrics in *Hold April*, even though they are propor-

---

7. This does not overlook that there are two volumes of selected poems. They will be discussed later in this chapter.

tionately few in number. More significantly, the combination leads to a serious consideration of the poem as medium for satire, the results of which have been collecting in "Birdland's Golden Age" since around 1965.

Stuart has come to recognize his fundamental proclivity toward prose rather than poetry. "In my youth," he writes, "most everything I did was poetry. Poetry (and its various and varied forms) were not big enough to carry all my ideas. So I turned to the story and the novel."[8] Although what he says is true, it is incomplete as an explanation. Since publication of *Taps for Private Tussie*, he has gone the way of success—the way which has continued to secure recognition. He has often confused media and genre. "Kentucky Is My Land" and "My Land Has A Voice," for example, were written as prose and later cast into lines. Conversely, he writes of *Album of Destiny*: "I thought the plot would make this book a novel in verse where colorful characters poured from every page."[9] When he first began writing stories, he confused forms: "I'm trying to write stories. I get moods for a group of poems. I put the words in prose."[10] Later in *Man with a Bull-Tongue Plow* and *Album of Destiny* he reversed the procedure, grouping poems to tell a story. "Behind each individual and each sequence in my poems," he contends, "there is a story."[11] More often than not, the individual becomes the voice narrating the story in the sequence. "Oh, What a Poem I Am In" is a good example of the poet's confusing genres:

> Laugh on you long-billed crane! Stand propped upon a Sandy River floating log! As long as you stand there you'll leave the little fish alone. Feathery, up on silken climbing wings—slow flying, up and up into the autumn rhythm until you are a part! And little homely shikepoke takes over where you stood—your leaving didn't break a heart!

8. Letter to the writer, September 9, 1969.
9. "Why I Think *Album* Is My Best," *Prairie Schooner* 30 (1956), 36.
10. See *Beyond Dark Hills* (New York, 1938), p. 378.
11. "Autobiographical Reminiscence," *University of Kansas City Review* 27 (October 1960), 59.

> Along my Sandy River
> The reeds and waterlilies quiver;
> The golden eyes of daisies plead.
> Soil, water, sun are all they need
> To spread a white and golden sheet
> Over a bottom for the tall cranes' feet,
> A flush green carpet for the tall cranes' feet.

> Away from water—away from Sandy River to my woods
> where tough-butted white oaks long have stood—tough
> trees that gather little sustenance from the clay—a stub-
> born tree that likes to have its way.[12]

Presumably, the poet is in the rhymed lines, although they are not extremely unlike what follows them, in which line equivalents are marked by dashes. Often refusing to make sharp and binding distinctions, Stuart has always possessed curiosity about ideas and how best to express them. Subsequently, one can surmise that the way of success has been enjoyable.

The title poem in *Kentucky Is My Land* is a prosaic tribute to the poet's native state. Written in free-verse paragraphs reminiscent of experiments in the juvenilia, it echoes the early influence of Carl Sandburg. More about the poet's Kentucky experience than about Kentucky, it is held together by structural metaphor: "If these United States can be called a body, / Kentucky can be called its heart" (p. 11). Beginning at the heart, geographical exploration of the country is metaphorically a physiological exploration of the human body. At the same time, "Kentucky Is My Land" has an Edenesque quality about it. A child (presumably the poet) is born into a pastoral world, and as he grows he comes to know it through his senses:

> Spring was in the wind.
> I could feel it.
> I could taste it.
> I could see it.
> And it was beautiful to me. (p. 12)

---

12. Enclosed in a letter to the writer, December 8, 1969.

If there is an overriding theme in the poem, it has to be the growth of consciousness. One is reminded of Whitman's "Self singing," an idea which is reinforced through long Whitmanesque catalogues of things seen, heard, tasted, smelled, and touched. Before going beyond his hills to explore the country, the poet reaches this conclusion:

> I knew more than ever before my brain
> Had been fashioned by the sights and sounds
> And beauties of wildgrowth and life of the hills
> That had nurtured my flesh from infancy to full growth.
>
> (p. 15)

He makes his sojourn, but metaphorically returns to the heart—to the organ most responsible for the life of the body.

Part II of the collection begins with "The Ballad of Lonesome Waters," which sounds like numerous other poems, and in which lines containing references to the "landlord's only daughter" sound like "The Highwayman," by Alfred Noyes. Others remind one of the anonymously-written "Sir Patrick Spens": "The caw-caw crow he laughed from his tall tree / And never a merrier haw-haw laugh laughed he" (p. 21). The ballad is about a young man who runs away after getting a mountain girl with child. There is an old saying in the area which goes like this: *In lonesome waters when you drop a dime, / It may be long but you'll return sometime*" (p. 25). After nine years the young man returns to find his lover married. A bloody fight ensues in which the husband is killed and the long-lost lover loses an arm. Although poorly written, the poem is intended as a domestic tragedy. Tone breaks down, with hilarious results:

> When Jim came home he pulled a gun on Dave
> But One-eyed Jim is sleeping in the grave.
> For One-armed Dave was fast for One-eyed Jim.
> He pulled his gun and got the best of him. (p. 24)

Although the title stipulates a ballad, the poet does not attempt ballad measure. Rhymes are forced and true. Lines are padded. And the language, far too much of it, is simply unbelievable.

Other poems in Part II are "The Cities," "Mountain Funeral," "Deserted Coal-Mine Camp," "Elegy for Mitch Stuart," and "By Sandy Waters." Like "The Ballad of Lonesome Waters," most of them were first printed in the Thirties and are therefore too close to the juvenilia to show anything new in the way of technique. "The Cities" appears to be of more recent vintage. Written in couplets, most of which are closed, it develops the old theme of William Blake's "dark Satanic mills." In stating his preference for rural life, the poet resorts to hyperbole: "I came back to ten thousand life-blood loves, / I came back to the high-hill earth to stay" (p. 27). The latter of the two lines, of course, contains the whole point of the poem. "Deserted Coal-Mine Camp," first published in 1952, is one of Stuart's many attempts to "hide the scars with loveliness":

> In years to come their mother mountain earth
> Will hide scars where these veins of coal ran thin;
> Bracken and fern will be a pretty wreath
> To hide the sunken spots where mines caved in.
>
> (p. 29)

Expressing a noble sentiment in traditional quatrains, "Deserted Coal-Mine Camp" is unusual for the poet only in the sense that it resorts to frequent off-rhymes: "here—Briar," "was—grass," "earth—wreath," "where—disappear."

Part III, "Songs for Naomi" (the poet's wife) returns to the sonnet and echoes Elizabeth Barrett Browning: "How can I do without you? I cannot" (p. 38). One also sees the parallels which characterize much of *Album of Destiny* in "A Song for Naomi":

> We work to fill our cellar and our bins,
> We work from spring until the freeze and frost;
> We work against lean hungry mountain winds;
> We work to find our labor is not lost. (p. 37)

Similar parallels are found throughout Part III. As love son-

nets, the poems are sentimental, containing nothing in the
way of technique which would particularly distinguish them.
"Wind Music" (p. 40) employs structural metaphor in which
the wind in alternate situations becomes different instru-
ments, but the device is an old one for the poet. Tone and tech-
nique in the entire section are probably best summarized in
these lines from "April Music":

> No plowman has a sweeter love than mine.
> No fairer love than my Naomi Deane.
> She climbs high hills beneath the oak and pine,
> I carry her across the streams between...
> She walks with me to hear the music in
> The April torrents and the pine-tree wind.
>
> (p. 37)

Part IV, "Poems for My Daughter," is overly sentimental,
and is occasionally given to moralizing:

> I think of families now torn asunder,
> Scattered and lost on roads with evil turning
> While we sit safely here behind log walls
> In warmth reflected from our wood fire's burning,
> Safe from the wind and rain that sadly falls.
>
> (No. 3, p. 46)

But in one respect "Poems for My Daughter" is the best work
in the entire collection. In sonnet after sonnet, the poet breaks
the ends of lines loose, creating a sense of movement:

> This life that we created stirs in dreams
> Tonight while floods of cold November rains
> Charge down these rugged slopes in roaring streams,
> And raindrops slither on our windowpanes.
>
> (No. 1, p. 45)

When he eliminates end-stops and places syntactic breaks
within the line, the result is a measure of freedom which is
almost totally foreign to *Album of Destiny*. In that sense, the

poems in Part IV are a fine example of relaxing what was earlier much too rigid.

Part V is entitled "Songs of a Mountain Plowman." It is the largest in the collection and contains a strange assortment of sonnets. There are poems about such modern conveniences as flying ("Up Silver Stairsteps," p. 62). And there are poems about times long gone by. "Their Ancient Love Is Written in This Dust" (p. 59), for instance, is about plowing up Indian relics. One thinks about Alfred Noyes' "The Barrel-Organ" when he reads of "green-up time" in "Spring Song" (p. 58), and about Ezra Pound's "In a Station of the Metro" when he looks at the beginning of "Railway Station, Joliet, Illinois":

> How many people have I seen like these,
> Impressive faces I shall see no more;
> These people pass like autumn wind-blown leaves,
> Their footsteps echo on the clean-tile floor.
> (p. 63)

There is a note of anti-intellectualism in "Independence" (p. 53), and another of skepticism concerning the consequences of modern technology in "Modernity": "But since I drive, my legs are losing power, / For clutch and brake are not leg exercise" (p. 65). For the most part, "Songs of a Mountain Plowman" is a celebration of life in the hills:

> This night a million stars pin back the sky
> To make a jewelled roof above this earth
> And I must go to hear the night winds cry
> Over these ancient hills that gave me birth.
> (p. 64)

The poet, traversing his "ancient hills," gathers images of his Appalachian heritage. Beyond that, there is little to be said.

"Great Lakes Naval Training Station" is the sixth part of *Kentucky Is My Land*. An autobiography of the mind, it contains an overwhelming obsession with place. It is like the preceding section, except that perspective changes. All of the images which were stored up now pour forth:

> I'll keep old images of time and place,
> Of redbud coves in fiery flakes of bloom,
> Curve of Naomi's lips, her handsome face,
> Jane's playing with blocks in our living room.
> Eternal churning of the sea can't break
> What I would sacrifice for freedom's sake.
> (No. 7, p. 82)

He obviously does not care for military life, but at the same time he possesses a sense of obligation to his country. Desperately homesick, he recalls sights and sounds from what he calls "this brain-embedded world of mine" and catalogues them. One finds no references to Great Lakes Naval Training Station, or to the navy, except for brief speculation that atolls must be very unlike Appalachian hill country (p. 81), and about what it might be like if the poet were ever lost at sea (p. 82). Far from home, he has one aspiration:

> To see these rugged hills of home again
> Before uncertain flight through troubled skies,
> To be where autumn wind sends down red rain
> Has brought me moods and hot tears to my eyes.
> (No. 1, p. 79)

Technically, the sonnets are like those of previous sections, containing nothing in that respect which has not already been discussed.

The last section of *Kentucky Is My Land* consists of one long prose poem—"The Builder and the Dream"—which is Jesse Stuart's dream of a post-wasteland America. The prose in which it is written is relatively free; at least it is farther from lyric than anything else in the collection. Ruel Foster's estimate is quite accurate: "Not a great or a good poem, it does describe a great and good act—an act potentially far more valuable than most poems."[13] As narrative, therefore, and not as poetry, the story of Ben Tuttle contains considerable interest. Foster is correct; Ben is a man of great deeds. Something

---

13. *Jesse Stuart* (New York, 1968), p. 70.

of a Don Quixote, he finally makes one of his dreams come true:

> And this, Ben Tuttle's dream, began with trees
> That they might grow again in this wasteland,
> And that his tiny checks for teaching school would buy.
> (p. 88)

Ben plants trees and grows a beautiful forest, one which people come from great distances to see. According to the poet, it is such a magnificent forest as this that mankind will need in the future—after the wasteland. Ben works in harmony with nature, and one does not have to guess what the forest means or symbolizes:

> He [Ben Tuttle] takes his place beside the dreamers
> And the builders of our human destiny
> Because he has produced a great forest. (p. 95)

The effort is curative, a way to restore spiritual health, and it is this which makes Ben Tuttle's act valuable for all mankind. It becomes a model for the spiritual restoration of America.

Jesse Stuart does not take a narrow view of his characters, and Ben Tuttle is no exception. Attached to the land, they gain their strength from it. Drawn away, they become sick and die. One suspects that Stuart himself is the model for Tuttle. He, too, is a dreamer, a writer, a teacher, a farmer, and a conservationist. Momentarily cast in an heroic mold, Tuttle becomes an instrument of the poet's vision, symbolically providing a way out of the wasteland. What the writer of the poem thinks of the character and the deed are clear: "He's done more than a general who leads / An army into battle for he has created" (p. 94). There is a geographical progression in the narrative, as well as in the deed. Both begin in Kentucky, move outward through Appalachia, and hopefully into the world.

After *Kentucky Is My Land*, ten years elapsed before another thin volume appeared. In the meantime, the poet suffered a severe heart attack, which probably proved to be the strongest influence on tone in *Hold April*. The boisterousness of *Man with a Bull-Tongue Plow* is missing. And even more than in *Kentucky Is My Land*, the poetry is relaxed. It could be that almost two decades proved sufficient for getting over the disappointment which came with publication of *Album of Destiny*. As though he were beginning anew, the poet places God at the center of the universe, probably indicating that his heart attack allowed him to solve religious crises which had been accumulating over the years. The skepticism which characterizes earlier work has diminished. The pessimistic naturalism of previous collections has given way to religious optimism. And the former morbid preoccupation with death is replaced by a quiet and gentle acceptance that life will be what it will be. More than anything else, *Hold April* is set apart by its quietude, which is doubtlessly what Robert Hillyer was referring to when he described the collection as "a beautiful book, a rare book, with its own golden place in our too-often shadowy literature."[14]

Although he has not given himself over to atonality, Jesse Stuart comes closer to "modern sound" in *Hold April* than in any of his other collections. In that sense, it contains proportionately more good verse than one finds elsewhere. Most of the poems were written in the late Fifties, after the heart attack. Of those previously published, three represent the Thirties, and there are none from the Forties. Unlike *Kentucky Is My Land*, there is no effort to group poems by affinity, no structural plan with division pages and other such paraphernalia. In more ways than one, therefore, simplicity and honesty become virtues in their own right, more so, at least, than one is accustomed to in any of the earlier poems. Not that the poet is usually dishonest; he is simply more aware of the need to be honest. Probably, that too is characteristic of quietude, of letting the song sing itself softly and sweetly.

Although placed in the middle of the collection, the poem entitled "Dawn" is undoubtedly the most important one be-

14. Found on the dust jacket of *Hold April*. At Stuart's request, Hillyer selected the poems which were finally published in the collection.

cause of the changing vision that it emphasizes. The poet rises from his sickbed and walks out into the world just before dawn. He goes at such a time because he wants to be alone, to take stock, to examine old habits and old attitudes. Looking through darkness and into a distant valley, he declares that this is the way to "summarize the world" (p. 56). There is something of a Swiftian view involved, for he sees the earth at dawn as an awakening giant, and himself as one of the little people. He has widened his vision, and in doing so has found his place, with which he is content:

> Joyously, happily, my heart full of love I walked
> To this high summit bringing with me
> Only the invisible parts of life's dreams that count.
> I brought love with me, understanding, tolerance,
> The curiosity of one's going where something is
>   about to happen. (p. 58)

"Dawn" ends with a reference to the poet's having come close to dying. With a new lease on life, he vows that his remaining days will not be spent in vain. Finally, he makes it clear that he has undergone a religious experience—a rebirth:

> I stood upon the threshold in my zero hour
> Wherein I witnessed a rebirth
> When God's own light dissolved in darkness
> In conflict for the final power. (p. 62)

The crisis of the heart attack brought him new modesty, and made the heart chief among his symbols. Ever aware of the weakened conditions brought on by a severe attack in 1954, and frequently reminded of it through a series of less serious ones since, he is acutely conscious of what it means to be mortal.

The poetry in "Dawn" is entirely another matter. It reads like second-rate prose. The usual end-rhyme has been dropped. Lines are jagged and uneven. Almost totally missing is the spirited lyrical quality which one finds in other poems, and of which the poet is quite capable. Far less pleasing tonally than the long prose poem "Kentucky Is My Land," "Dawn," notwithstanding, belongs to that impetus toward prose which has made *Hold April* the last book to be published, other than the selected poems.

"Love Song After Forty," although placed first, is not the most accomplished. Expressing warm and beautiful sentiments about married love, it is technically akin to "Dawn." At its best, it resembles modern mode:

> The second ledge has views that are sublime—
> Where drowsier mumbling bumblebees
> Put their last accents on the wasting flowers,
> Where a mountain daisy blooms beneath the thyme,
> Until plucked by this hand to fasten in your hair.
>
> (p. 17)

The word "plucked," used for "picked," sounds archaic, but the recurrence of sibilants, as well as voiced and unvoiced stops, holds the lines together. Laterals are also prominent. Still, considered at its worst, "Love Song After Forty" is indeed bad:

> Unbored,
> We have soared
> On levels where life's patterns run—
> Springtime with blossoms in our eyes,
> With the bright wings of butterflies,
> And summertime with growth and sun,
> A time to shape and mould the things undone.
> Unbored, we have soared,
> Until older, yes, but none too wise,
> For we have starlight in our eyes. (p. 17)

The first two lines will offend any trained ear, and to repeat the pattern is to double the insult. Part of the difficulty lies in the fact that the thousands of sonnets written in the prime of his career in no way prepared the poet for anything like this. Rhyme creeps in unwanted, as do parallels and other reiterative devices. Nor did the sonnet as lyric form prepare him for writing long narrative poems. Even when his early sonnets were written in sequence for purposes of narration, the story told was loosely connected, largely lacking in transitions. "Love Song After Forty" is not as obviously narrative as "Dawn" or "The Builder and the Dream," but it is not substantial lyric either. Therein lies its major weakness. Caught in limbo between two traditions, it conforms to neither, and the reader comes away convinced that it is too severely flawed technically to stand on its own.

Considering the length of Jesse Stuart's career as sonnet writer, one would expect the short lyrical poems in *Hold April* to be the most accomplished. "Green River," which is typical, flows with relative ease:

> Green winter river flowing to the sea
> Between snow-covered banks and barren trees,
> I speak to you and you speak back to me
> With interruptions of a winter breeze.
> In seasons past my love and I have stood
> Beneath your willow, elm and sycamore
> And hummed tunes to the music of your flood,
> And written lyrics to your lilting roar. (p. 30)

Measured and rhymed, lines correspond to syntactic breaks, but there are no awkward starts and stops. Nor is there the usual raking against the nerves; sound is euphonious. One finds more off-rhymes in *Hold April* than anywhere else in the poet's work. Examples such as this are frequent:

> Never was night as wind-swept beautiful!
> Blow by them winds, in deep poetic mood!
> Go whine among the sedge where cidia lull,
> But do not chill poor circulating blood.
> (p. 39)

There are other reasons why *Hold April* is potentially Stuart's best, and most of them can be found in "Autumn Sequence," consisting of six free-flowing sonnets. In the first place, the form is the one in which he is widely experienced.

Secondly, diction is colloquial but modern; clichés and archaisms are missing because he has discarded the voice of the rustic hill man. In doing so, he has also dropped the first-person stance, resulting in greater distance between the poet and the poem. Thirdly, the numerous reiterative devices which characterize *Album of Destiny* are greatly relaxed. Grammatical parallels, for example, do not impose themselves rigidly upon the lines of an entire poem. Confined to two or three, instead, they are relatively infrequent. Rather than trying to control tone from outside the poem—and even from outside the individual line—he has found that he can gain more control from within, and all the time remain inconspicuous. Even where parallels appear, they seem less rigid because of sounds which work from within:

> Approaching autumn wind makes lizards stir
> And sleepy snakes seek hibernating hole,
> And drowsy scorpions search for sun somewhere
> And dizzy wasp return to oaken bole. (p. 40)

One suspects a misprint. Surely, "wasp" should be plural. On the other hand, the string of sibilants dominates sound structure. Releasing the ends of alternate lines, and at the same time creating a slight offset in the rhyming of "stir" and "somewhere," the poet reduces an effect which would otherwise assault the sensibility of the reader.

All in all, one comes away from *Hold April* with highly ambiguous feelings. It is good, and at the same time it is bad. The poet has released himself from overly-rigid form, but he has not accepted irony, paradox, allusiveness, and other characteristics of modern mode. In some instances, he is close to atonalism; in others he is far from it. The major weakness of the collection as a whole can probably best be explained by a demonstration from within one of the poems. "The Two Houses" (p. 35) is structured metaphorically. In it there is a house of life, and one of death. Between the two there is a great gulf or void. Such is the case, also, in *Hold April*. In the house of life, poetry has been freed from earlier rigidity of form; in the house of death, it has not. The early poems—"Desolation" (p. 88), "House in the Wind" (p. 78), and "The Ballad of the Bride" (p. 92)—should never have been included. In all three, meter is far too regular (sing-song); diction is faulty; rhyme is heavy and regular; and in "Desolation" in particular one has to question the poet's seriousness. "Old Christmas" (p. 101) is equally inferior. Purporting to be a dramatic dialogue, it possesses most of the same faults. Written in duples and heavily rhymed, "Of Dead Leaves" (p. 76) is plagued with awkward starts and stops. "Free Ride" (p. 72), about a Texas fly catching a plane ride to Chicago, is frivolous.

On the other side of the gulf—in the house of life—are songs that sing themselves. Included among these are "Song" (p. 20), "Time Passes" (p. 22), "Autumn Poem" (p. 24), "Green River" (p. 30), "Spring Voices" (p. 34), "Autumn Sequence" (pp. 38-41), "Come Gentle Snow" (p. 45), "Sandy Will Flow Forever" (p. 51), "The Snow Lies Patched" (p. 54), "Soliloquy of the Wild Rose in the Rock" (p. 67), "World of Springtimes Past" (p. 83), "Hold April" (p. 87), "Voices of Spring" (p. 91), and "Be in a Joyful Mood" (p. 106). These poems are lyrically successful, possessing vitality and movement. Still, while going through *Hold April*, the reader—shuttled back and forth between the two metaphorical houses—soon learns that its most serious fault is unevenness. The poet has moved far from his practices in *Album of Destiny*. As a result, grounds for assessing the poems have also shifted. While it probably is not entirely fair to hold them up to expectations of modern mode, neither is it justifiable to base an assessment on the poet's old techniques. Finally, admitting that there are difficulties in finding suitable criteria for purposes of evaluation, it is quite obvious that entirely too much dross remains.

Jesse Stuart has in his possession an unpublished manuscript consisting of poems written in the early Thirties. "Songs of a Mountain Plowman" belongs to the period that produced *Man with a Bull-Tongue Plow*, and because pro-

sodic technique in the two is highly similar, it deserves no
further consideration in that respect. Being recently assem-
bled, however, "Songs of a Mountain Plowman" has consid-
erable value because the poems included, as well as how they
are arranged, reflect definite attitudes on the part of the
poet. With publication of *Hold April* (1962), there came
another impasse. Rooted in tradition and refusing to budge,
Stuart's next major poetical effort would consist of writing
satire. There is precedent for such a practice in his fiction.
The novel *Foretaste of Glory* (1946), for instance, is an ac-
count of a massive confession of human foibles and
weaknesses brought on by fear of the aurora borealis. Hora-
tian satire, the story is loaded with humor and good fun.
There is also precedent in the poems, particularly in *Album
of Destiny*. Saurians, wind, and grass all reflect upon the
place of mankind in the universe, constantly exposing his
arrogance, greed, and inconstancy. "Songs of a Mountain
Plowman" is helpful in understanding the poet's interest in
satire. A new arrangement of old material, it allowed him to
bring past and present together in one manuscript.

Consisting of four parts—"Sonatas of Spring," "Songs of
the Summer Sun," "Songs of Approaching Autumn," and
"Songs of the Silent Snow"—the typescript sets forth once
again man's existence in terms of the old death-rebirth ar-
chetype. One does not read far until he discovers that the
poet has rejected contemporary values, and that he is search-
ing the past for values which can endure in the present. In
effect, he sees himself in a wasteland, no longer a part of
America "that used to be." He admonishes poets to sing, be-
lieving that singing (art) is the only surviving means of
creating values worth bothering about:

This is your time to sing, there's only one
Time for to sing your song and that is now.
Sing under the bright light of autumn sun,
Of yellow springtime sun behind the plow.
This is your time to sing while the ox cart

Is rotting in the chipyard and the cattle yoke
Decaying in the woodshed of dry-rot.
This is the time to sing songs of your heart;
You see America that used to be is fading, fading
    to eternity.[15]

He celebrates his ancestry, and refuses to accept the "chang-ing world." About those Americans who have lost their love for land, he writes:

The path they found is easier than the plow
But it takes beauty from the brain and heart
And kills men's spirits that would play a part. (p. 17)

As in *Man with a Bull-Tongue Plow*, there is mutability in all things, and man necessarily comes to a naturalistic end:

It does not matter, death is only change.
Now kill the flesh, if you can, in this man,
This flesh will live again in something strange.
            ("These Same Dead Leaves," p. 21)

The daughters of strong pioneer stock have taken to whoring and drinking wine (p. 6). Made soft by their easy pleasures, they can no longer give birth to "stalwart sons." Hence, the race weakens:

Great sleepers you, I feel that we have strayed
Away from paths that lead us to the known,
That we are growing weaklings half afraid. (p. 8)

Having watched the decay of his country, the poet is desper-ate. A creature of the wasteland, and trapped within it, he is limited to making vain boasts:

America! America! America!
By hell, I say you will go on and on!
America! America! America!
By hell, we'll pilot you through cleaner dawn.
                    (p. 27)

---

15. Untitled, p. 15. Most of the poems in "Songs of a Mountain Plowman" are untitled. Further references included in the text.

More than anything else, "Songs of a Mountain Plowman" is a manuscript of old poems reflecting recent attitudes. In it, the poet constructed himself a summary of the past. And having done that, he immediately set about making projections concerning how best to deal with the future.

"Birdland's Golden Age," Stuart's collection of satirical poems, had its inception around 1965. Unlike anything he has ever written before, it is radical, but only out of need. It is controversial, but only because the times are sadly and pathetically out of joint. Having cultivated the sonnet form for thirty-five years (longer than that if one considers that *Harvest of Youth* was published in 1930), he is for the first time willing to abandon it. And having made his Kentucky hills almost exclusively his subject matter, he is willing to go beyond them. The long-cultivated lyrical strain gives way to narrative, proselike commentary, and the voice of the rustic hill man is silenced. Looking back to *Kentucky Is My Land* and *Hold April*, one realizes that they conspicuously relieve the poet of old commitments, and at the same time avoid subjecting him to new ones. As a consequence, in "Birdland's Golden Age" he uses his art to launch direct attack upon social, political, and moral ineptitude.

Jesse Stuart has always been impressed by the verse satires of John Dryden and Alexander Pope, but he also knows that seventeenth and eighteenth century satire looks back to its Roman beginnings. When queried about his knowledge of Roman satirists, he responded: "Catullus, among the Romans, was a poet of satire. He lived about thirty years. He was a great satirist in about 114 poems left to posterity. I've read Horace, Juvenal, and Catullus."[16] The poet's metaphorical birdland may have its origin in Aristophanes' play entitled "The Birds," but its immediate impetus is to be found in present madness of the world. Specifically, the bird poems began out of anger over the way President Lyndon Johnson handled the war in Vietnam: "If the man, President Johnson, who started my bird poems had done what Goldwater

---

16. Letter to the writer, May 30, 1972.

suggested, or what President Nixon is doing now, there would never have been these bird poems."[17] Once he had begun writing them, however, he found that he could not stop. The madness, he discovered, did not stop with the Johnson administration. Indeed, it continues into the present: "In a way, we're still living in Birdland. Wallace now shot. Wilt (The Stilt) Chamberlain, a millionaire because he's seven feet three inches tall. This could only happen in Birdland."[18]

In "Read Me and Love Me," Part I of "Birdland's Golden Age," the poet is mostly concerned for cultivating an audience and an atmosphere. References are almost exclusively to himself, his audience, and his newly adopted practice of writing satire. At the outset, he establishes subject matter and method:

> Who will accept the poems
> In my newborn book?
> This time, am I alone
> To give this book to you?
> Will thousands accept them?
> Will thousands own this book?
> Will a million read it
> In my reedless, loveless land?
>
> The self-appointed judges,
> Big Winds and Little Winds,
> Who blow to Washington,
> Who blow from Washington,
> Who blow in Washington
> To show their importance
> Will censure what I say
> In poems I have wrought
> Recording fun and frolic
> Of our own L.B.J.,
> Our own great god Apollo,
> Our everybody's man,

17. Letter to the writer, May 16, 1972.
18. *Ibid*.

> Our true composite man
> In our Great Society.[19]

As the history of satire indicates, it probably belongs to an
age of prose. At its best, it is a way of being subtle—even
polite—in time of oppression. Whether the present age is
ready for satire or not remains to be seen, but once again
Jesse Stuart looks to the past for a way of handling contem-
porary problems. With emphasis on "This time," lines three
and four of the above seem to imply that previous efforts
have failed because of interference. But this, he tells the
reader, is a new start. He is being facetious in lines six and
seven, but that is essential to establishing satirical tone as
preparation for the second stanza.

The poet sees himself and others as dehumanized: "I am
a name and a number. What are you?" (p. 4) He makes clear
his need to communicate: "I talk because I am alive, / Be-
cause I have something to say" (p. 8). He compares his com-
ing satirical attacks to those conducted by missiles, and in
doing so elaborates upon his plan:

> What potency has poetry
> With which a missile can be filled,
> More power than block-buster bombs,
> More power than atomic bombs
> To change the wrong to right on earth
> And not spill blood and leave a scar.
> ("My Missiles," p. 10)

The purpose—changing "wrong to right"—remains essen-
tially what it has always been. The method, by contrast, is
quite different: "Announcing phoney birds in flight / Before
they sink us into night" (p. 10).

Jesse Stuart has his doubts about such a radical change
in method. He is afraid of losing the lyric impulse once and
for all. Paradoxically, though, his sense of moral responsibil-

---

19. Untitled, p. 1. The entire manuscript is in Stuart's possession in
W-Hollow. Further references included in the text.

ity will not allow him to remain silent:

> Don't let them dim
> My lyric light
> And push me back
> Into the night.
>
> I must attack,
> I must be true;
> All-out attack
> Is overdue.
>> ("Don't Let Them Dim My
>> Lyric Light", p. 14)

Willing to sacrifice present popularity for a just evaluation in the future, he perceives that there is no turning back:

> Someone, I tell you, will
> Remember me years hence
> I think and I'll be saved
> By the judgement of good men,
> I who have been oppressed
> By the fear of oblivion.
>> ("You Are Wrong When
>> You Say It," p. 18)

Part II, entitled "Don't You Worry," begins with an attack on President Johnson. "How Like the Great Greek God Apollo Is Our King," which has been published, decries the vanities of self-seeking and bathing in unearned glory.[20] Satire depends for its effect upon such devices as irony, innuendo, hyperbole, and incongruity—all of which the poet knows and uses. In one instance, political aides and advisors become buttons on a god's robes:

> Never you mind, he'll trust White Buttons yet,
> To hide scars prominent everyplace,
> To make our homeland clean and lily white.
>> ("Apollo's Buttons," p. 26)

---

20. *Esquire* 64 (December 1965), 242.

Treating that which is significant in terms of such trivia as buttons, he counts on contextual connotations of "lily white" to reinforce satirical tone. The attack on President Johnson continues in "The President and I." Cast in the mold of a god, the president walks on the surface of a pond, which is hardly the place for divinity. With his godlike attributes, he creates wealth without labor, and with one grand gesture of his hand banishes poverty from the entire country (pp. 28-32). The method, of course, is that of caricature, and the results are ludicrous.

Other people are satirized in Part II. Evangelist Billy Graham, for example, is taken to task in "Big Names in the News." Before the poet has completed with him, Graham is dressed in Joseph's "coat of many colors / Unmindful of his surgery and death" (p. 38). In "Knock! Knock! Who's There?" Graham pays a visit to "Lovely Lady Bird" at the White House, where angels are "ordinary things" (p. 39).

In Part III, Mrs. Johnson's beautification program is satirized:

> O Lady Bird, Our Mother Bird,
> Make beautiful our nest for us,
> Tear down the signs and sow the flowers,
> We trust you know what's best for us.
> ("Our Mother Bird," p. 56)

Beside the overriding metaphor of birds in the nest, the last line is derisive and loaded with irony. In the same section, President Eisenhower is described as a bird who "flopped his chance" because he ended the war in Korea:

> He sacrificed his reputation,
> Eight years of Love and Dream and Peace,
> And a little white ball on the Green.
> ("Why Dwight D. Eisenhower
> Was a Failure," p. 53)

In "Birdland's Club of the Immortal Feathers," Billy Sol Estes is another of the poet's objects of "fun and frolic." Be-

cause he "rubs feathers with Chief Eagle Bird," he is as-
signed a place among the club's illustrious membership. To
all of those who do not belong—birds of lesser stature—the
poet dedicates "To Be Forgotten Winds":

> You small to be forgotton winds
> I'll give you immortality
> When you're enrolled in my new verse,
> A week, month, year, maybe, forever;
> You tell me what you think is worse
> Than being in my book to be! (p. 108)

Entitled "Four Maidens and a King," Part IV of "Bird-
land's Golden Age" is directed at President Harry Truman's
decision to drop atomic bombs on Nagasaki and Hiroshima.
In "Our Little King," set twenty years after the bombs were
dropped, the reader is introduced to a "little ordinary fellow"
who must live with his conscience:

> No wonder he can't sleep at night!
> He wakes to fiery consummation
> At midnight in some flaming town,
> In Hiroshima, Nagasaki,
> At midnight hours he fights the flames.
> (p. 114)

The reader is next introduced to the four maidens, one at a
time, and is shown how the bombings ruined the lives of
each. With Misako Kannabe (pp. 117-119), one looks back
twenty years to the time when she was sixteen and beautiful.
But the bombs came, and Misako crawled home to find that
there were no doctors and no medicine. Toyoko Minowa (pp.
120-123), at age eighteen, also survived the holocaust, but
remains as helpless after forty operations as she was then.
Michiko Yamaoka (pp. 124-126), badly burned, crawled to the
beach to die. Kept alive through a series of operations, she
has never been fit for marriage. Suzue Oshima (pp. 127-130)
crawled home so badly burned that her father did not know
her. "Four Maidens and a King" undoubtedly contains the

most accomplished satire in "Birdland's Golden Age." One can come away from the poet's treatment of Mrs. Johnson and Billy Sol Estes, for example, feeling that he is really being petty. But in "Four Maidens and a King," the reader's sympathies are genuinely touched, forcing him to share in guilt which rightfully belongs to all Americans—not solely to a lonely little man who can not sleep at night.

In Part V, "Lonnie and the Local Winds," Stuart returns to his home state, satirizing the "Local Winds," and particularly Kentucky's one-party political system. In Part VI, "Appalachian Suicide," he once again takes up writing his unorthodox sixteen-line sonnet:

> This is the place of desolation here,
> The mines have fallen, tracks have rusted red;
> The lizards, rabbits, crows are left to care
> Where shacks have tumbled and the damp is dead.
> Life once was here: one couldn't ask for more;
> Mole-men, fat cheeks, for mining our black gold
> Stepped sprightly all night on the dance-hall floor,
> Unmindful that tomorrow's camp would fold.
> What of tomorrow when there was today,
> And hell with those who spoke of waste and sin;
> John-L was god who upped their take-home pay,
> They whored and fought and drank highridge and gin.
> Then unexpectedly there came the blight,
> An economic fungus over all;
> There came Depression's endless lonely night
> Recorded by the blacksnake's writhing scrawl.[21]

Besides addressing himself to practices of strip-mining which have denuded Appalachian hills, he attacks federal programs for their inadequacy in relieving poverty. A visit to Appalachia by President Johnson is singled out for special treatment:

---

21. Poems from "Appalachian Suicide," including this one, have been published in *Esquire* 72 (December 1969), 104.

> A tall man with Disciples of his Creed
> Swarmed in like flies to shake "poor peoples' " hands,
> Cameras clicked, the tall man spoke of need:
> *No poverty like this in all the land,*
> *A billion dollars will cure all your ills.* (p. 181)

In the last section of "Birdland's Golden Age," the poet continues his concern for a world which has gone mad:

> We seek the new sunrise to change a world
> That has grown mammon sick, immoral, evil!
> ("Impression Eight," p. 198)

He challenges America's youth to make themselves heard above what he refers to as "this nauseating chatter." Believing that democracy is in desperate need of being purified, and contending that the greatest threat comes from within, he calls for an end to violence and murder. In "Bores and Cutworms in the Lineage Trees," he concludes with this warning:

> The little bore can kill
> The stalwart stalk of corn
> From the top down
> Instead of bottom up;
> The cutworm hidden in the ground
> Can snap the silken whitehair roots
> To wither blooming flower shoots.
> (p. 227)

Since publication of *Hold April*, Stuart has directed his attention primarily toward writing fiction, although he has continued to write and publish poetry. Other than writing satirical poems, his poetic efforts fall primarily into two categories—publishing and republishing old poems, and publishing those which have come out of his travels and experiences abroad. The latter, escaping geographical limits of Appalachia, take for their subject America and the world. Outside the poet's role as chronicler, as are many of the satires, they pose certain problems. Because of subject matter alone, they could be interpreted to mean that the poet has finally given up on the idea that he can influence both the world of art and the real one through his microcosm. The recent fiction, however, because it continues the chronicle, would not substantiate such a view. Whether the larger stance will eventually threaten continuity of the chronicle remains to be seen.

Among those poems reprinted are "Lincoln Weeps," from *Harvest of Youth*, and "Love Song After Forty," from *Hold April*.[22] There are others which appear to be of earlier vintage but which are not included in any of the poet's collections—at least not before the selected poems in 1975. These include "Ballad of John Winslow," long and written in couplets; "Shinglemill Symphony," consisting of eight sections of four quatrains each; and "Love-Vine," written in couplets, most of which are interlocking.[23] Occasionally, an editor writes requesting poems, and Stuart's practice has been to send them when circumstances permit. Of considerably more interest, however, are the poems about America and the world. In 1960-1961, the poet was visiting lecturer and professor at American University, Cairo, Egypt. In 1962-1963, under auspices of the Bureau of Educational and Cultural Affairs of the Department of State, he made a world lecture tour. In 1966, he spent the summer in Europe and on the Mediterranean. And in 1969, he toured the African continent, visiting sixteen countries. Throughout his travels he has looked for educational and cultural contrasts—a context in which he can view his own country and a yardstick whereby he can measure its progress.

One would expect such intense scrutiny to be reflected in the poet's art. The trips abroad appear to have increased his

22. For "Lincoln Weeps," see *The Angels* 5 (Spring-Summer 1968), 5. For "Love Song After Forty," see *South* 3 (Fall 1970), 9-16. The title is changed to "Lovesong for Over Forty."
23. "Ballad of John Winslow," *Hawk and Whippoorwill* 1 (Spring 1960), 5-7. "Shinglemill Symphony," *American Forests* 71 (December 1965), 28-29. "Love-Vine," *The University Review* 32 (1966), 218.

love for his native land, even though he is painfully aware of its internal problems. Proud of his heritage, and grateful for his freedom, he celebrates America in song:

> America, when I awoke I found you
> And you became my source of honest song!
> America, I found your greatness 'round me;
> I must sing well of you.
>   I must sing long.
> Your mighty mountains are my place of birth,
> Your rivers I have known since life began;
> I know, also, your miles of fruitful earth,
> I plowed them long before I was a man.
> Your earth is in my heart and brain and blood,
> I am of it and it is all of me.
> Your moaning wind has given me a mood!
> Free as your blowing wind I have been free.
> America, I am awake to sing
> Of you since you are my immortal song.
> I shall sing loud of you.
>   I'll make hills ring!
> I shall sing well of you.
>   I shall sing long![24]

Lines such as these lend support to the idea that he is serious about his satire, and that he views himself as one who is fulfilling a much-needed function. Although educative and relaxing, his wanderings have made him keenly aware of what he has at home.

The poems coming from trips abroad register impressions, and frequently show the poet making judgments. For instance, in "Up-to-Date Identity" he chides modern Greeks for allowing cultural decline:

> Young modern Greeks will you tell me
> Your up-to-date identity,
> Departure from your ancestry

---

24. "America, When I Awoke I Found You," unpublished and undated. Found in Box No. MS-69-1 in Stuart's personal library.

To restauranteers and bartenders
For the world: is this your aim in life?
Where are your citadels of learning?
Your schools of philosophic thought?
Milleneums ago you reached
Heights when each great Greek was a teacher!
Your schools were filled from all the world
And learning's light was your bright star.
Today your star is overcast—
Not even sanitation in
Your Greece where medicine first grew.
Your visitors now take away
Not germs of thought but other kinds
That rise up from your ancient dust
To plague two million visitors.
Now I am anxious to depart;
Land that inspired, inspires me no more.[25]

It is obviously an old and ancient Greece which has inspired Stuart—the god Apollo, the early theater, and the rich merchant fleets. In "Delos by the Sea," he passes ancient Greece in review, dismissing modern Greece as a case of "Immortal loneliness."[26] In considering Ephesus, city of pagan ruins in Asia Minor, he also exalts the superiority of that which is ancient. "Only the dream is left," he concludes.[27]

Having praised America's past throughout a long writing career, and having praised in particular the Blue Dreamers in Plum Grove Cemetery (burial place of pioneer stock near Stuart's house), the poet seems unwilling to appreciate any country for its present existence. Typically, in "Where Pindar Lived" Thebes is important because it is the home of Pindar, and even more so because the W-Hollow poet views Pindar as a conservative man, one who was reluctant to accept change:

Pindar: spiritual unity of Greek art;

25. Unpublished and undated. Found in a box labeled "Foreign Poems" in Stuart's personal library.
26. *Cincinnati Pictorial Enquirer*, Sunday, May 21, 1967, p. 12.
27. "Dry Wind of Ephesus," *Arizona Quarterly* 25 (1969), 347.

Pindar: conservative who could not change
Whenever growing Greece changed in his time;
Four and twenty centuries have passed
Since Pindar walked these streets in ancient Thebes,
And centuries before, his ancestor,
God Cadmus, founded his immortal Thebes.[28]

There are poems about other cultures, and in all of them the poet expresses his need to know about the past. The same inquisitiveness characterizes "Korea to the World":

Koreans, tell us about yourselves!
Shout to the world about Korea!
Why imitate small Literatures,
Indefinite schools of thought?
Koreans, tell us about your culture
Older than our America![29]

In Iran he finds an old way of life still intact, over which he is enthralled:

How poetry is respected in Iran,
It's chanted by the farmers in the field,
Quoted by those who cannot read or write,
Yes, poetry is their culture to the bone.[30]

He writes about Egypt in general and Cairo in particular in "Where April Sings":

The Pyramids keep vigil on the sand,
They've seen five thousand Aprils come and part
From a jasmine and a lotus scented land
Where Egypt is an image in each heart.[31]

Here, too, one finds Stuart's concern for loving one's country—a love which is made stronger through a knowledge

---

28. *Caravel: A Magazine of Verse*, No. 14 (Fall 1965), p. 33. Volume number not given.
29. *Korea Journal* 3 (July 1963), 13.
30. "Where Angry Winds Blow," *Poet Lore* 63 (Spring 1968), 29.
31. *Snowy Egret* 31 (Spring 1967), 21.

of its past. In these poems, as in his production ranging over the years, the past is poetic because it inspires the best thoughts and deeds of men in the present.

The World of Jesse Stuart was published by McGraw-Hill in 1975.[32] As a first volume of selected poems, it does not purport to advance anything new in the way of technique or craft. Rather, assuming the poet's home in W-Hollow as a geographical center, each of the seven sections of poems in the book moves farther from that center in subject matter than the one just before it. Section titles should be self-explanatory: "The World as Self Singing," "The World as Song Singing Itself," "The World as Springtime Kentucky Hills," "The World as Appalachian Desolation," "The World as Ship of State," "The World as Journey to Ephesus," and "The World as Universal Brotherhood." The object of such a method of organization is twofold: To avoid the chronological approach characterizing nearly all such collections, and to place the emphasis on the fact that ultimately Stuart's concern is anything but provincial. His growth has been a geographical one in that even the poems with a W-Hollow setting have come to be more and more about the human condition in general, and about the human condition in America in particular.

The World of Jesse Stuart contains poems reprinted from all of Stuart's collections. It contains poems reprinted from journals and magazines, and it contains some from unpublished manuscripts such as "Birdland's Golden Age" and "Songs of a Mountain Plowman." It also contains poems which are not from such manuscripts, but which nevertheless have not been printed previously. Dedicated to displaying the range of the poet's work, the volume contains lines cast from his prose, such as "Kentucky's Night Winds" (p. 156), as well as the best of his lyrics, such as "Green River" (p. 56). All in all, the poems selected for *The World of Jesse Stuart* bear out the idea that Stuart is a chronicler-poet, whether he is at home in Kentucky or off in some far corner of the world.

---

32. *The World of Jesse Stuart: Selected Poems*, ed. J. R. LeMaster (New York, 1975). Further references included in the text.

The Seasons of Jesse Stuart was published in 1976.[33] The second volume of selected poems, it is an autobiography in poetry. Capitalizing on the structural plan in *Album of Destiny*, the book contains seven sections: "Youth," "Struggle," "Summer," "Success," "Rebirth," "Travel," and "Autumn." Although *Seasons* contains a Foreword by Stuart, each section is introduced by a short biographical essay, written by the editor. Reprinted from *Man with a Bull-Tongue Plow*, the first poem in the book is intended to explain the plan of organization:

> Man's life is like the season of the flower.
> From barren earth in Spring the flower comes forth—
> A flower springs to blossom and decay.
> The Spring is but the season of its youth
> And then it blossoms to the wind and sun.
> It blossoms forth and stands in fresh array—
> Stands in the pride and beauty of its day.
> But soon, too soon, these petals know decay,
> When Spring has gone quickly the summer goes.
> Then autumn frosts and then the winter snows.
> The flower's season is the life of man.
> Spring is the season for his youth and growth.
> Summer is when maturity puts forth.
> Autumn brings ending to his futile dreams.
> Winter: he's numbered with the dead-leaf stems. (p. 3)

Supporting the idea of the chronicle in every conceivable way, *Seasons* is a large book with an unusual format. There are 230 pages measuring 11½ by 8½, each containing two copies of the same poem—one hand-written and one printed. It is an effort to be personal, the hand-written copies are in the poet's large scrawl, and must have taken weeks to prepare for reproduction. There are also photographs in *Seasons*— photographs of Stuart and his family, each accompanying an appropriate poem. More about the man than anything else,

---

33. *The Seasons of Jesse Stuart: An Autobiography in Poetry*, ed. Wanda Hicks (Danbury, Connecticut, 1976). Further references included in the text.

Seasons is the autobiography in poetry that it claims to be.

As the acknowledgments indicate, many of the poems in *Seasons* have been printed elsewhere. Stuart explained in a letter dated February 14, 1977, however, that the book contains a few poems which he thought to have burned in the dormitory fire at Vanderbilt when he was a student there. He explains the circumstances: "I worked at the Sixth Street Shops, American Rolling Mills then, Armco now, and Mr. White was superintendent of this part of the American Rolling Mills. He was an unusual man and took a great interest in me. I gave him extra copies of my poems, which he kept. At this time I had never seen a college campus."[34] That would have been shortly after the young poet graduated from Greenup High School in 1926; he was a freshman at Lincoln Memorial University during the school year of 1926-1927. Of *Harvest of Youth* vintage, the poems that Stuart had thought burned were returned to him recently by Margaret White Rigsby, daughter of the man for whom he had worked in the steel mill. In his letter he names two of the poems from *Seasons* as belonging to that group—"Crossroads" (p. 7) and "Goodby to Yesterday" (p. 8).

One should not expect a volume of selected poems to contain anything astounding. But the fact that two such collections were published within 24 months of each other, 13 years after his last volume of poems, may indicate a renewed interest in his poetry. In these two volumes of selected poems, as in all of his preceding collections, one remains impressed that his poems are attempts to crowd out the strictly modern, that which has lost its identity with the past. In the selected poems, too, the poet's task appears to be what it has always been. As Jesse Stuart sees it, the poet inspires noble thoughts and noble deeds. Through keeping men in touch with the best from their heritage, he leads them, one by one, to a more perfect humanity.

---

34. Letter to the writer, February 14, 1977.

6

The Beauty of Words:
A Concept of the Image

A detailed study of Jesse Stuart's imagery would be necessar-
ily long and involved. Such a study would have to consider
tree imagery, bird imagery, flower imagery, crop imagery,
animal imagery, water imagery, images of evil, images of
death and sterility, and various kinds of images having to do
with both birth and rebirth. One need not go into such detail,
however, to find important and basic assumptions underlying
his concept of the image.

First and foremost, it is essential for him, as it is for
William Carlos Williams,[1] that imagery lie somewhere in the
interreliance of man, nature, and thing. For the artist, it is
indeed in things that the power of the image lies. Stuart at-
tempts to lift his Appalachian locale to the level of poetry, and
images come spontaneously and naturally from the environ-
ment. The reader could just as well be transported and set
down in the middle of W-Hollow, for that is the effect which
the poet hopes to achieve through his imagery—imagery
amounting to sensuous encounter resulting from his early
and elementary fascination with words.

Archibald MacLeish says that a poem begins in "the *Wen*

---

1. Linda Welshimer Wagner, *The Poems of William Carlos Williams*
(Middletown, Connecticut, 1964), p. 31.

Fu, not in isolation but in relationship."[2] In other words, the poem is something that "traffics" between man and his milieu. MacLeish quotes one of Mallarmé's letters to Degas: "Poetry is not made with ideas: it is made with things or words that signify things."[3] For MacLeish, as for Mallarmé, poetry is made of words themselves, of words as sensuous events, which are necessarily double constructions: "They are sounds which are also signs for meanings and signs for meanings which are also sounds."[4] MacLeish recognizes a necessary marriage between phonetic or phonemic content and morphemic or word content.[5] In the elementary linguistic sense implied here, language is highly sensuous. The sound and the sign combined make the word, and neither can exist without the other. Knowing this, says MacLeish, a poet "goes to the 'things' of the world not to have thoughts *about* them but to discover them and so to discover himself looking at them."[6]

In a qualification, Mallarmé contends that poetry is either made by things or by words that signify things. The difference seems to be a crucial one; at least it does for John Crowe Ransom:

> An idea is derivative and tamed. The image is in the natural or wild state, and it has to be discovered there, not put there, obeying its own law and none of ours. We think we can lay hold of the image and take it captive, but the

---

2. *Poetry and Experience* (Cambridge, 1960), p. 6. MacLeish is using his background in Chinese poetry. He is specifically echoing a *Fu* by Lu Chi, a poet-general who lived around the end of the fourth century and the beginning of the fifth. The *Fu* is a prose poem written about literature, and in particular about the poet's art. MacLeish uses Lu Chi, he says, because Lu Chi "speaks to our condition as contemporary men" (p. 4).
3. *Ibid.*, p. 22.
4. *Ibid.*, p. 29.
5. This is taking into consideration the usual definition that a phoneme is the smallest element of structure making a difference in the larger structure of the stream of speech, and that a morpheme is the smallest element that makes a lexical difference.
6. *Poetry and Experience*, p. 21.

docile captive is not the real image but only the idea, which is the image with its character beaten out of it.[7]

Ransom is talking about a physical poetry with a "thing" content, but words are not physical things. Very early in his career Stuart made these observations: "I wanted to put thoughts into words. Words were living things. Verse was living words combined to make a living body and a living force that would be felt" (BDH, p. 219). The emphases are on words, on things, with the characteristic feature of living—"living words," "living things," "living body," and "living force." He obviously wanted life in whatever it was that he considered to be the task of the poet, but was confused. Regardless of how much life there might be in words, he knew that words and physical things were not the same: "Words are marvelous things. They are something which you can do anything with but take hold of with your hands" (BDH, p. 34). He knew what he wanted, but he did not know how to get it.

Stuart tries to shake loose from words and "stand naked" in a world of things. In *The Year of My Rebirth* he begins with things and attempts to work back to the poem: "This grass is a poem. Each blade is a letter, a clump is a strong, selective, poetic word. This yard, an oasis of tender green, is a small spring lyric."[8] He has persisted in asserting that poetry exists in things—beyond words. These lines from an early story sufficiently illustrate where the poem is, and what the poet's task is:

Life is here, music is here, love is here. Poetry is here in the music of the wind in the saw-briars and the great magnificent sweep of dead leaves that cover the earth now. There are thousands of lines of poetry in the wind here. It is poetry that never grows old. One only has to

7. "Poetry: A Note On Ontology," *The World's Body* (Port Washington, New York, 1964), p. 115.
8. P. 65. Perhaps because it was written while he was recuperating from a near-fatal heart attack, this journal contains some of his most profound observations about life and art.

take a pen and copy the melody from the wind, the words from the earth. It is life here, great life.[9]

The melody comes from the wind and the words belong to the earth, but for the poet the melody of the wind and the words of the earth are living things. As the rhythms of the four sentences indicate, he was trying to "copy" in some way, even though he knew that his efforts were futile, that the image tamed is not an image at all but an idea.

Stuart has mailed to the writer one of his numerous attempts to "stand naked" in a world of things. It is a five-page typescript, which is written in poetic prose. As an effort to capture or arrest the poet in a world of autumnal things, the typescript is significant not only because it is an affirmation of his obsession to get beyond or behind language, but also because its very execution illustrates once again that the language of good prose, as far as he is concerned, is essentially the same as the language of good poetry. The first paragraph places the poet within the autumnal world:

The whole earth around me now is in rhythm. It is an autumn poem with rhythmic measure. Autumn, fast winds, slow winds and no winds accent this physical poetic masterpiece! Try walking in and on and over a poem like this just one time! Hear it changed! Get full of it, as I am now, and see if you can describe how you feel! You just try putting autumn's poetic rhythms into words.[10]

The autumnal poem is a poem of "rhythmic measure," with rhythms that are wholly natural and harmonious. It is a "physical poetic masterpiece," beyond ideas and beyond words. At this point, it makes Jesse Stuart sound like Samuel Taylor Coleridge, who says that "nature itself would give us the impression of a work of art, if we could see the thought

---

9. "Ascension of Autumn: A Rhapsody," *The Southern Literary Messenger* 1 (January 1939), 18.
10. "Oh, What a Poem I Am In," unpublished typescript enclosed in a letter to the writer, December 8, 1969.

which is present at once in the whole and every part."[11]

On the first page, the poet places himself in the forest. The second page continues the autumnal experience there— one of trees, birds, winds, and leaves. The birds become "periods to hold poetic lines on this poetic autumn earth." Any section of the typescript can be cast into lines by simply following the pauses:

> Here are the slopes of sterile earth—
> covered with sedge—good old brown broomsedge—
> a cover for the rabbit, grouse and quail.
> And all this sedge is now a-quiver—
> in autumn rhythm that cannot go on forever.
> Trees in motion, falling leaves—
> winds that laugh and winds that grieve
> winds that make the sedgegrass quiver—
> autumn winds, yes, autumn winds
> that can't go on forever.

The slopes of sterile earth, the quivering sedgegrass, the falling leaves, and the trees in motion are details that an artist painting an autumn scene would surely have on his canvas. One need only follow the dashes, marking breath-units, to realize that a poet's control over his imagery lies inevitably in his control over language. The essence of Stuart's concept of the image is here, as is the essence of his concept of prosody.

The images continue throughout the poem: tough-butted white oaks, leaves on the skin, wrinkles in the water, cranes, shikepokes, and buttercups. The sketch ends with the poet's affirming once again his place in "autumn's rhythmic rhyme." It is, he writes, "a part of me and I a part of it—this poem since my birth." The leaves splashing in the face may convey "poetic messages," and the poet may imagine birds and leaves to be dots and dashes punctuating "this earth's big poem," but he knows that the poetry cannot be lifted from the earth. Because the rhythms belong to the flowing of water, to the flight of

---

11. "On Poesy or Art," *Modern Criticism: Theory and Practice*, ed. Walter Sutton and Richard Foster (New York, 1963), p. 37.

birds, to the swaying of trees, and to the functions of all natural phenomena, they cannot be lifted from the earth either. Subsequently, riding the rhythms of these natural things, images are bound to the earth. Stuart would agree with Ransom that the image is wild in nature and cannot be tamed.

To "stand naked" in such an autumnal world is not to write poetry. Rather, it is to be in poetry, to be of poetry, or perhaps even to be poetry. Whatever the case, it emphasizes the poet's problem. For him poetry appears to be in things, although Mallarmé says that it may be in words that signify things.

Ralph Waldo Emerson first published his optimistic, idealistic philosophy in *Nature* (1836). In explaining his philosophy he stated a formula that goes far in accounting for Stuart's concept of the image. He says 1) that words are signs of natural facts; 2) that particular natural facts are symbols of particular spiritual facts; and 3) that nature is the symbol of spirit.[12] Emerson sees the world in terms of emblems, and considers all of nature to be a metaphor of the human mind. By the time he published "The Poet" (1844), he had extended and clarified his philosophy considerably. In that essay he declares the poet to be a Namer or Language-maker. He says that every word was once a poem, and that every new relation is a new word. The poem itself he explains as "a thought so passionate and alive that like the spirit of a plant or an animal it has an architecture of its own, and adorns nature with a new thing."[13]

Stuart's God-in-nature mystique, his view of man in nature, his penchant for animating trees, grass, and other things in nature, along with such metaphors as that of the grass in *The Year of My Rebirth* and that of the poem in "Oh, What a Poem I Am In,"[14] all tend to identify him with Emerson's formula, and to make him similar to the ideal poet of

12. *The Complete Works* (Boston, 1884), I, 31.
13. *Ibid.*, III, 15.
14. The metaphor is structural or functional, and the entire poem is a metaphor. For a discussion of symbolic metaphor see Wagner's *The Poems of William Carlos Williams*, pp. 47-48.

Emerson's essay. His much-used expression that images are in the "album of the brain" also appears to be emblematic. It is likely, in spite of the proposed identification, that he did not borrow his concept of the image from Emerson. He did not borrow it, directly, from anyone. As indicated earlier, he had an obsession with Walt Whitman about the time he attended classes at Vanderbilt. By then he had read the King James Version of the Bible. He had also read widely. One finds vestiges of all the great nineteenth-century English writers in his poetry, as well as vestiges of nineteenth- and twentieth-century American writers. As indicated in Chapter 1, he has asserted that he consciously copied no one. He did not copy Emerson; nor did he copy Whitman. He, in his overwhelming fascination, simply absorbed Whitman, who happened to have been heavily influenced by Emerson. T. S. Eliot, in "The Music of Poetry," explains the kind of thing that took place:

> it is only the study, not of poetry but of poems, that can train our ear. It is not from rules, or by cold-blooded imitation of style, that we learn to write: we learn by imitation indeed, but by a deeper imitation than is achieved by analysis of style.[15]

Eliot is talking about versification, but not about that alone. The "deeper imitation" amounts to a level of absorption on which such things as versification, imagery, and structure cease being distinguishable from each other.

From the earliest, Jesse Stuart has been attracted by the sister arts of music and painting. In *Man with a Bull-Tongue Plow* (1934) he is "a farmer singing at the plow" (p. 3). His prose and his poetry contain remnants of church hymns, square-dance calls, and numerous references to music in natural things. His people, he reports, sing the old ballads that have been handed down for generations, and each of them tells a story. He was not trying to escape his sources of song in 1932 when he worked out a plan for *Album of Destiny*. The idea of painting pictures, outlined in his defense of that

---

15. *On Poetry and Poets* (New York, 1957), p. 19.

book,[16] is in effect an effort to make greater use of the sources. The photographs found in the family album were very much like the images on the "album of the brain" in that both were illusions of a sort. The details were in the pictures also, and they were vivid. Using the idea of creating illusions, he set out to "picture" his W-Hollow milieu. Each picture would be contained in a single poem, and the whole gallery, taken in the four seasons of the year, would create illusions of W-Hollow on the one hand, and Man in the universe at large on the other.

It was at this point that Stuart found Whitman useful. Whitman had gone to Emerson for his theory and attitude toward words, and had encountered such ideas as these: 1) "Bare lists of words are found suggestive to an imaginative and excited mind";[17] 2) "Nature offers all her creatures to him [the poet] as a picture-language";[18] 3) "The etymologist finds the deadest words to have been once a brilliant picture. Language is fossil poetry."[19] Whitman, using Emerson's ideas about picture-language and lists of words, set out to inventory the universe, to name it into existence. His catalogues are long lists that both sound and signify. Locked in each word, Whitman thought, is the vicarious experience of the poet, the opportunity to know life or Being in all of its details. Showing an obvious Emersonian influence, Whitman's attitude toward words is treated in the twenty-fifth section of "Song of Myself." The attitude is also dealt with in "Poem of the Sayers of the Words of the Earth" (1856):

> Earth, round, rolling, compact—suns,
>   moons, animals—all these are words,
> Watery, vegetable, sauroid advances—beings,
>   premonitions, lispings of the future,
> Behold! these are vast words to be said.
>
> Were you thinking that those were the words—

16. "Why I Think *Album* Is My Best," *Prairie Schooner* 30 (1956), 32-34.
17. "The Poet," *Complete Works*, III, 22.
18. *Ibid.*, p. 18.
19. *Ibid.*, p. 26.

> those upright lines? those curves, angles, dots?
> No, those are not the words—the substantial words
>   are in the ground and sea,
> They are in the air—they are in you.[20]

"Poem of the Sayers of the Words of the Earth" invites comparison to Stuart's "Oh, What a Poem I Am In," and to any number of his poems and prose selections. The birds that dot the sky are periods in the poem—which is not on paper but rather is explicable in terms of Whitman's doctrine of inner and outer meanings. Whitman's "vast words to be said" can just as well be sung or chanted, as Whitman himself illustrates in "Song of Myself." T. S. Eliot, also, has observed that the poem consists of one person talking to another, and that singing is simply another way of talking.[21] Whitman chants the names of things to produce a particular emotional effect in the reader, one corresponding in some rough way to the emotion of the chanter or singer. The words chanted are stimuli, each having its referent in the emotion of the reader.

Gay Wilson Allen believes that the discovery of the catalogue method marks the beginning of Whitman's new system of prosody.[22] Whether this is the case or not, Whitman came to think of himself as a painter of pictures. Specifically, he expressed emotion either by naming the sensations of which the emotion consists, or he indirectly portrayed the emotion by naming the concrete objects which can be counted upon to produce the sensations.[23] The objects named in Whitman are usually simple and concrete, and he mostly names the object without attempting to describe it further. He took great care in choosing his "magic words."

Richard Maurice Bucke collected and published a volume of Whitman manuscripts, many of which reveal Whitman's

20. *Leaves of Grass*, 1856 Edition. Quoted in Gay Wilson Allen, *Walt Whitman Handbook* (New York, 1946), p. 433. In the 1881 Edition the title was changed to "Song of the Rolling Earth" and the first three lines were dropped.
21. "The Music of Poetry," *On Poetry and Poets*, p. 23.
22. *American Prosody* (New York, 1966), p. 236.
23. *Ibid*.

intentions—stylistic and otherwise. Bucke printed four lines
of Whitman's "Pictures" in his collection:

> O Walt Whitman, show us some pictures;
> America always Pictorial! And you Walt Whitman
>   to name them.
> Yes, in a little house I keep suspended
>   many pictures—it is not a fixed house.
> It is round—Behold! it has room for America,
>   north and south, seaboard and inland, persons . . . [24]

"My Picture-Gallery" is dated 1880, and appears to be a revision of the lines from "Pictures":

> In a little house keep I pictures suspended,
>   it is not a fixed house,
> It is round, it is only a few inches from one side
>   to the other;
> Yet behold, it has room for all the shows of the world,
>   all memories!
> Here the tableaus of life, and here the groupings
>   of death;
> Here, do you know this? this is cicerone himself,
> With finger rais'd he points to the prodigal
>   pictures.[25]

The "little house" sounds much like Jesse Stuart's "album of
the brain." It is obviously the mind, and the images collect
there for dispersal. Whitman's pictorial method consists of ar-
ranging his words into lines or verses in such a way that each
line or verse presents a picture of some characteristic scene,
event, group, or person.

Emory Holloway has also been interested in Whitman's
pictorial method, and has made some observations about his
finished "Pictures":

> Each is a microcosm of the whole *Leaves of Grass*, which
> the author looked upon less as a book than as a picture of

---

24. *Notes and Fragments* (London, Ontario, 1899), p. 27.
25. *Complete Poetry and Prose* (New York, 1948), I, 355.

himself in all his cosmopolitan diversity. And the more we learn of the facts of Whitman's comprehensive life, whether experience, reading, or meditation, the more we realize that before each thumb-nail picture was set down on paper it had really been hung, as a personal possession, on the walls of his "Picture-Gallery."[26]

Turning to Emerson's theory of symbols, Whitman apparently identified his own ego with the creative processes in nature, and through vicarious exploration of all forms and levels of existence he evolved his technique of panoramic imagery.

The ultimate question is what all of this has to do with Stuart. The answer is complicated, but it is also rewarding. What the poet has written in and about *Beyond Dark Hills* shows that he early knew the value of painting scenes. His term paper for Edwin Mims was full of scenes carefully executed. About doing the term paper he writes: "Blindly I beat the words out. They fell like drops of blood. I beat them with a hammer to make them paint the small pictures I have gathered in the album of my brain."[27] The "small pictures" which he says he has "gathered," and which exist or are stored in the "album of my brain," convince one that he was thinking and talking about imagery via the picture. His method was from the beginning pictorial, relying on his command of words to execute scenes. He knew Whitman well by the time he wrote *Beyond Dark Hills*, as his writing of the long poem "Whispering Grass" indicates, and what he says about pictures sounds remarkably like Whitman's pictures suspended in "a little house" which is "only a few inches from one side to the other." Stuart knew that the word as sound was sung or said, but as sign it proved to be another matter. The image, he discovered, can only be lifted from the "album of the brain" by singing or saying words that signify very concrete things.

This is not to say that images other than visual ones are

26. *Pictures* (London, 1927), pp. 10-11. See Holloway's Introduction for the importance of the image in Whitman's style.
27. *To Teach, To Love* (New York, 1970), pp. 159-160.

slighted. Indeed, a picture may evoke all of the senses. Such being the case, imagery in general is dealt with in Chapter 7. Nor is it to say that Walt Whitman is the sole influence on Stuart's interest in the visual image. As indicated in Chapter 1, the poet early tried to write like an Imagist: "An Imagist poem had to paint a picture or have an action in each single line. I was influenced by the Imagists. I thought it was the thing to do."[28] He considers the following lines—written at Lincoln Memorial between 1926 and 1929—to be "one of the most typical Imagist poems I have written":

Dreams of an Empty House

Late in the evening
Curtains of silver dew
Move ghost-like about this empty house,
This old pine-pole house
Down in the valley
Of head-high oats.

The scattered yard-flags bloom
Where the woodpile used to be.
The ramble rose vines climb
Up the rock ruins
Of a tumbled-in cellar,
And the clustered hollyhocks
Sway in the wind
By the smokehouse door.

Three stone gallon fruit jars
Hang on the garden palings
And a house wren builds her nest in one.

Late in the evening
The harvest moon
Rides high in the rag-bag clouds
Above the deep valley of head-high oats,
Rides high above the empty house that speaks.

But it may be the wind that speaks,

---

28. Letter to the writer, May 17, 1972.

The wind combing the tall yard grasses
And stirring the ramble rose vines.
It may be the wind worrying
The weather-cupped shingles.
And swinging the unlatched doors
On rusty hinges.

But anyhow, I hear my mother's mother
Singing "I'll Be All Smiles Tonight"
And "Nellie Was a Lady."

She lived here fifty years ago
And set our ramble rose vines.
She carried tin pails of milk
Over a flat stone walk
Into the tumbled-in cellar;
She canned apples in the fruit jars
That hang on the garden palings.

And in this cottage small
My mother lives.
She planted ramble rose vines
And sang "I'll Be All Smiles Tonight"
And "Nellie Was a Lady."

So the drowsy world of looking back
Paints a picture on the eyes,
Hammers thin music on the ear drums.

Oh, drowsy world of looking back
When "Nellie Was a Lady"
Into realities of dreams.[29]

   "Dreams of an Empty House" is rather unconvincing. Too frequently it reads like awkward prose: "Three stone gallon fruit jars / Hang on the garden palings / And a house wren builds her nest in one." Sounds are forced: "The ramble rose vines climb / Up the rock ruins / Of a tumbled-in cellar." Syntax is distorted: "And in this cottage small / My mother lives."

---

29. Enclosed in a letter dated May 17, 1972. According to the letter, "Dreams of an Empty House" was published in *Letters*, a University of Kentucky literary quarterly, in May of 1932.

And the poet resorts to poetic diction: "Curtains of silver dew /
Move ghost-like about this empty house." With all of its faults,
the poem is interesting because of what it attempts, because of
its subject matter, and because it identifies Stuart with the
Imagists. It deals with concrete objects found in his rural Ken-
tucky, and with his never-ending pride in ancestry. Of most
significance, and rightly so, are lines such as these: "So the
drowsy world of looking back / Paints a picture on the eyes, /
Hammers thin music on the ear drums." The reference to "a
picture on the eyes" looks forward to his concept of the album,
which provided both the structure and the method for *Album
of Destiny*.

The poet experimented with his scene-painting, and
found his prose to have the sweep of good poetry:

> Mellow is the wind
> and yellow are the leaves
> and yellow is the mist
>   about the pools
>   of leaf-strewn water.
> Scarlet are the leaves
> and scarlet are the patches
> of shoe-make woods
>   in the pasture lands
> and the snow-briar stools.
>
> Almost.yellow is the tobacco
> and yellow is the corn,
> but scarlet the cane tops
> and the cane blades.
> The earth is scarlet and yellow.
> Look at it!
> The whole earth
>   around us
>   is scarlet and yellow,
>   the waters
>   and the mists
>   and the briars
>   and the trees!

Yellow the noonday September sun,
scarlet the setting September sun
and scarlet is the sky
around the setting sun.[30]

Stuart's concept of the image is closely bound to his philosophy of Being, and nowhere is this pointed out more effectively than in *Kentucky Is My Land* (1952) and *Hold April* (1962). Although neither collection makes a significant contribution to advancing his practices concerning imagery beyond the point he reached in *Album of Destiny*, each contains valuable insight into his thinking about the image, the word, and the poem.[31] In "Kentucky Is My Land," a title poem, one encounters again the idea of poetry as sound and picture, existing somewhere beyond words:

The lonesome streams in the narrow-gauged valleys,
Sang poetic songs without words.
And the leafless trees etched on gray winter skies
Were strong and substantial lines of poetry.[32]

He concludes the poem by declaring that "bluegrass beauty" is not akin to poetry, but "is poetry." He also declares, as he does in "Clay from the Heart of It" (p. 60) and numerous other poems, his belief in the essential oneness of all things. Each refrain of the wind is poetry, and the poet may be man or oak:

---

30. BDH, p. 261. This is one of sixteen prose scenes in *Beyond Dark Hills* (New York, 1938) that I have cast into lines. Nothing has been changed; even punctuation remains the same. In some instances Stuart himself has recast his prose into lines and published them as poetry. He says, for example, that "Kentucky Is My Land" and "My Land Has a Voice" were both written as prose and later cast into lines (Letter to the writer, October 3, 1969).
31. *Kentucky Is My Land* (New York, 1952) is especially interesting because of the two long prose poems in it—"Kentucky Is My Land" and "The Builder and the Dream." They are illustrations of the poet's idea that both good poetry and good prose must be succinct and directional.
32. *Kentucky Is My Land*, p. 14. Further references to KIML included in the text.

Today, I am the master of this tree,
To chop it down, to split its fibered seams;
Tomorrow, Plum Grove oak will cover me
And its tenacious roots will break my dreams.
("The Plum Grove Oaks," p. 61)

Robert Hillyer, an acquaintance of Stuart's, writes of the dreamlike quality of the poem.[33] The poem for Hillyer is dream-stuff. For Stuart, it is not the poem that is dream-stuff; it is life. As in "The Great White Silence" (p. 67), we live in the dream we are dreaming. In "Summer Has Faded," summer is "a written book that we have read" containing "sentences of green beneath blue skies" in which each word is "now a leaf of dying red" (p. 66). In poem number six of "The Last Leave Home" the poetry is in "this brain-embedded world of mine" (p. 82). The long poem "The Builder and the Dream" is an account of Ben Tuttle's building the dream in which he lives. Nature is Ben Tuttle's model; he "looked to Nature's book for guidance" to build his dream (p. 89). He listened to the "voice of Nature speak," and read "her message" in the sky, in blades of grass, and in flowers (p. 92). His dreams, we are told, "were great in childhood" (p. 85). As it turns out, the greatest of his dreams is to build a dream-forest in which to live. Stuart here defines the relationship of the poet and the dream—also referred to in "Dreams of an Empty House"—about as well as it can be defined. In "This February Night" he has the water speak to the poet:

Record your little rhyme for those asleep
For spring will wake soon after February
And winter unrecorded will not keep.
(p. 66)

As in "The Great White Silence," the poet lives in and is a part of poetry. According to the water in "This February Night," his job is that of the chronicler; he records the dream.

---

33. *First Principles of Verse* (Boston, 1950), p. 18.

Jesse Stuart is obviously serious in his attempt to "stand naked" in a dream-world. The poems in *Hold April* indicate that he is. In "Two Leaves" he writes: "you and I are two leaves drifting by" in the wind.[34] In "Be in a Joyful Mood" he adds that the "highest mind today is not enough," for we are "part of all this harmony" of the universe (HA, p. 106). "Small Wonder" is a miniature "Song of Myself" in which the poet celebrates his essential oneness with the earth, and about which he says: "I am a part" (HA, p. 104). His "gladness of the earth" is that of being at one with the earth, of being in the dreams. In "Boy or Calf" it consists of being somewhere between "the birth of bud and fall of leaf" (HA, p. 69). In "Dawn" it is a matter of being an "infinitesimal, borrowed part" of "transitional earth" (HA, p. 62), of being a "living portion of earth's flesh" and "a kingdom within myself" (HA, p. 60). The idea of essential oneness is perhaps best stated in "Man and His Valley":

> I do not understand
> Infinite wisdom of this workable plan
> That everything is oneness with the land,
> When you are valley and I am the land.
> (HA, p. 26)

Because he does not understand those "wordless blueprints from eternity," he explains in "Why Ever Grieve," he relies on Nature to "reproduce the broken parts" and make them whole again (HA, p. 21).

In "Summer Writes Another Book," the season is "a linguist who writes in many tongues" and holds the pen of the poet (HA, pp. 28-29). Morning glories, growing up stalks of ripened corn, are "lyric poetry in this book." Rows of corn, cotton, and wheat stubble are "strong, substantial sentences." There are also "structural sentences in the sky / And on the lonesome leaf." The poet, according to his own theory of Being, is in the morning glories, the stubble, and the leaf, and they

---

34. *Hold April* (New York, 1962), p. 107. Further references to HA included in the text.

are part of him. Thus it is difficult to talk about him as though
he is a thing apart, and about the poem as though it has rec-
ognizable boundaries.

The poet's emphases on life as dream-stuff, his brain-
embedded world, is in itself sufficient reason for his finding
Walt Whitman appealing. With Whitman he says, "the sub-
stantial words are in the ground and in the sea, / They are in
the air—they are in you."[35] Ben Tuttle's dream-forest should
be considered among Stuart's major attempts to "image" the
mystery of Man's Being, but the nature of the dream for all
men, caught up in the mutability of all things, is perhaps best
summarized in "Hold to a Living Dream":

> Remember stones will crumble, dirt will loose
> An avalanche of dream in tender spring
> To bud and flower into a luscious fruit . . .
> Winter, this dream will not be anything.
> Only your dream has value and can last,
>
> (KIML, p. 54)

His comprehensive portrait is that of Man caught up in the
flux, coming and going with the seasons of the year, and there
is only the dream—the world in the "album of the brain"—to
be recorded.

In the final analysis, Stuart's concept of the image be-
comes a matter of metaphysics. Transcendentalism via
Whitman is obvious, but one wonders about his concept of re-
ality. All things—like the tree in the forest that does not fall
unless someone sees or hears it—apparently exist in the mind
or not at all. The peculiar thing about such an idea is that it
has to be true; at least it has to be true from the viewpoint of
any one individual. When a man dies, the universe dies with
him. The image is always on the "album of the brain" of a man
who is alive. It is at this point that Mallarmé and the Chinese
poet Lu Chi make sense, as do Walt Whitman's "pictures sus-

---

35. *Leaves of Grass*, 1856 Edition. Quoted in Gay Wilson Allen,
Walt Whitman Handbook, p. 433.

pended" in a room large enough for all of the "shows of the world." It is the point at which the poet kicks loose from the earth long enough to view himself among the things of the earth, and in doing so takes time to imagine what the things of the earth would look like without him. Stuart's method is pictorial because he too has imagined what the things of the earth, and particularly the things of his W-Hollow milieu, would look like without him.

7

A Record of the Dream: The Image in Practice

In using the pictorial method, the poet does not limit his appeal to the eye. The picture may appeal to any or all of the senses. Jesse Stuart seems to have learned this gradually, as indicated by his early tendency to speak of the poet-singer and the poet-painter as being exclusive of each other. There is a progression in his development of the pictorial method, and with that progression there is an acceptance of the mutuality of what he early considered to be separate roles of the poet.

The poems written before his discovery of Walt Whitman, high school and undergraduate poems in *Harvest of Youth*, contain convincing experiments in versification and prosody.[1] By contrast, his experiments in imagery often fail. For instance, "Undulated Season," an overt attempt to write like an Imagist, is one of the more successful experiments. Section four paints an autumn scene:

> nasal Autumn
> tweaking winds in bare twigs
> plum leaves in a golden shower
> rustle with the wind
> down alleyways

1. The usual distinction between the two is that verse is metered language.

> called time
>> birds fly to bare plum twigs
> to chat of love
> one by one they come
> remembering the glossy green
> of their season
> mating (p. 29)

"Railroad Sounds" is another fairly successful poem, and largely because the poet does in it what he later learned to do well. That is, he makes reference both to the sense and to the object. Throughout the poem he repeats "I have heard," and he follows the repetitions with such expressions as "groans of heavy engines," "drive wheels slipping," "the lonesome whistle screaming," "oozing steam from slick pistons," and "the swinging and banging of box car doors." "These sounds," he concludes, "I have loved" (p. 31). The imagery in "Vagabond Houses" depends on metaphor. The houses are "Aged vagabonds / Resting by a road," and they are "Black drops of ink / Resting by a road" (p. 33).

Some of the most successful imagery in *Harvest of Youth* is found in the third section, "Sonnets: Juvenilia." Again it is made effective by naming both the sense appealed to and the object:

> Nocturnal things have been my loves: moon-downs,
> Valleys of fog and sleepy mountain towns,
> Dew on the grass and play of wind upon
> The hill. Night sounds I have loved: the cold
> Nosing winds in November corn stubbles;
> The zoom of wires and water that troubles
> Creek mosses and ferns.
>> ("My Loves Will Remain When I Have Passed," p. 47)

There is nothing sophisticated about such imagery. It is simple and direct. It sometimes comes via the symbol, and the symbol remains just as simple and unsophisticated as the thing symbolized. Stuart, for example, often uses the river as a symbol of life: "And a river young will wear a way to go /

Until it cuts a channel to the sea" ("Batter Me Down, Life,"
p. 48). In "A Skeptic's Plea" he simply lists or enumerates:

> If there is life beyond this life, let it
> Be this: The friendly Earth my boyhood knew
> With quaint old upland peach trees in the dew;
> High wind, a gust of rain, a shattered bit
> Of Heaven in a sleepy willow brook; (p. 53)

He is naming the objects in his milieu; dew-covered peach
trees do have a certain sensuous appeal, as does a willow-
covered brook. The poet often uses a simile: "And like Indian
Summer leaves, our life days burn / With candle flames"
("Louise," p. 56). He also uses personification, metaphor, apos-
trophe, metonymy, synecdoche, and other devices of duality
commonly used by all poets. They help to get the images be-
fore the reader, and in doing so lend structure to the poem.

Because the interest in Whitman began around the time
Stuart was at Vanderbilt, one would expect *Man with a Bull-
Tongue Plow,* done immediately after Vanderbilt, to show evi-
dence of that interest. The poet himself has described *Man
with a Bull-Tongue Plow* in terms of the senses: "The book was
finished, dreams and sights and sounds and feeling that would
not come again" (BDH, p. 375). The collection is important not
only because of what it contains of his practices concerning
the image, but also because it records the initial stages of his
attempt to reconcile the poet as singer with the poet as
painter. Not until *Album of Destiny,* though, does he reconcile
the two roles to the extent that he stops talking in terms of
either/or.

In *Man with a Bull-Tongue Plow* he conducts what ap-
pears to be a running commentary on his role as poet, and
although there is no assurance that the poems are arranged in
any particular order, the progression of comments does reveal
his shifting concept of himself from that of singer *or* painter to
that of singer *and* painter. After the initial identifications in
the first three sonnets—the farmer poet, his subjects, and the
nature of his song—there is an apparent groping or probing

for the craftsmanship that characterizes *Album of Destiny*. At the outset the poet is very much the singer: "This land is mine, I sing of it to you" (p. 6). The singer of land is also the singer of people: "These are my people and I sing of them" (p. 20). He knows the nature of his song: "The song is in my heart enough to sing, / A little song to fit this pasture world" (p. 36).

The next group of references in the commentary pertains to words. "My words," he states, "are wind-words lying on the land" (p. 74). Earlier he has said to his father that they "are facts as stars are facts" (p. 29). One cannot place his hands on the stars either. The rhetorical figure, as far as words are concerned, indicates much about Stuart's attitude toward them. The star and the word are beautiful, but both remain for the most part mystifying. The next reference to words concerns what the poet does with them: "Trying with words to mock a bird that sings" (p. 114). As indicated here, the job of the poet is to reproduce the bird's song, not to write about the bird.

From the beginning of *Man with a Bull-Tongue Plow*, references to the poet's art diminish in number, and throughout most of that collection he practices his craft without commenting upon it. Not until near the end of the book does he resume his commentary. There, in the last section, he presumes himself dead. He is, as a dead man, looking back at his life and art. The posture of the dead man, nonetheless, allows him to make a significant summary of his life and work. He addresses the earth:

> Earth, I have come to play my little part
> Among the lowly folks, for I belong
> To them—it is for them I sing my song;
> It is for them I give my rustic art.
>
> (p. 313)

Many of the poems near the end of *Man with a Bull-Tongue Plow* are addressed to Donald Davidson, who presumably has not died. To Davidson, the poet attempts to justify his art:

> Once, Davidson, I went to you with lays;
> I read you plow-boy lays no man had heard;

I read you lays of my kin's rustic ways;
I read old tunes to you like a fluting bird.
(p. 338)

At this point, he remains a singer, affirming that his subject
matter has not changed.

The final references in *Man with a Bull-Tongue Plow* are
not to song. Quite appropriately, they are to the poet's words,
which are used in sketching, drawing, and making pictures:

No Sir, I never tried to write a book.
My pencil traced the sounds of high winds blowing
And sketched a willow-aggravated brook
And made some pictures of the green grass growing;
Word-drew a peddler in a thread-bare suit;
Word-drew a new moon piece of cleared ground;
It pictured oak-brown leaves and red plum fruit;
White windy skies and water's lonely sound. (p. 347)

The concluding reference also concerns the poet's words. In it
he is still trying to justify his art. Further, he is defending
himself against accusations concerning his borrowings:

Don Davidson, if I have stolen words
To write in books, you must erase my name;
For words to me were big as skies to birds
And rhymes beat in my head hot as a flame.
Don Davidson, I did not ask them come.
But I sat by the plow and wrote them down.
I rhymed them to the slow beat of a drum
And to the whirs of dead leaves drifting down.
Why should I steal my words from books, I ask?
I carried brains and baskets filled with words;
I spun my rhymes—(To me it was no task)—
Words were to me I've said as skies to birds.
If ever I stole words from some dead poet,
Since I am dead I do not want to know it. (p. 348)

The shift in emphasis is from song at the beginning of *Man
with a Bull-Tongue Plow* to the picture at the end. In either

case, Stuart recognizes that the word is the artistic medium. By the end of the book he is obviously thinking of his W-Hollow gallery. In practice, *Man with a Bull-Tongue Plow* proved to be a book of adjustment. The art of picturing explored there is finally perfected in *Album of Destiny*.

The images in *Man with a Bull-Tongue Plow* are produced primarily in four ways: 1) by naming the sense appealed to and sometimes the object referred to, 2) by using symbols as well as various rhetorical figures or devices, 3) by placing objects in a context and naming them there, and 4) by simply naming objects in lists or catalogues, producing a panoramic effect.

The sense appealed to is often named in a simple statement: "I love to hear the foxes slipping by" (p. 206). There are numerous examples of the poet's loves and hates. He hates, in fact, "to see a dead rat in the rain" (p. 207), and loves "the smell of dead leaves in the rain" (p. 207). He loves to hear the "sounds of rabbits' feet upon dead leaves" (p. 335). There are also images of touch: "I love to break the tall weeds with my feet / And tramp pokeberry stalks and cresses under" (p. 131). In another place he adds: "We walk barefooted on mulch in the fields" (p. 7). He feels and smells dead oak leaves (p. 149). He places his hands upon "green, growing weeds," and finds his life in touching them (p. 126). His cornfield images appeal to a number of senses:

> When jewelled-dew drips from the blades of corn
> It's fine to hear a fresh breeze oozing through,
> Filled with the fragrance of the silking corn,
> Kissed by the dew a-dripping from the corn— (p. 8)

The following account of an experience in the woods is filled with images of touch, sight, and sound:

> I put my hands against your leaves and feel
> The tender ribs that hold heart-shapes to leaves—
> I kick the last-year dead-leaves with my feet;
> I put my hands to cold green bark on trees.

> I hear the willows swishing in the wind;
> I see the white clouds floating in the brook;
> I see September's leaves now drifting in
> The briars— (p. 143)

Jesse Stuart writes in the first person, and in *Man with a Bull-Tongue Plow* the poet and the man are never far apart. The man also delights in sensuous encounter with the natural things of his rural Kentucky.

Rhetorical figures and symbols in *Man with a Bull-Tongue Plow* are numerous. The imagery, therefore, depends heavily on similes, metaphors, and symbols, and these often make use of commonplace objects. For instance, stones are "dishpans with their bottoms up," and a quarter moon is a "brass drinking cup" (p. 105). Elsewhere the moon is a "block of white-ash wood caught in the leaves" (p. 160), and the poet, presuming himself to be dead, is "a gray stone lying in the grass" (p. 168). Dogwood trees are ships which "spread their white sails" (p. 70), and the grave is "Earth's jail-house behind the heavy doors" (p. 314). The wind is a "blowing bellows" (p. 277), and death is an "uninvited guest" who drives a surrey pulled by two black horses (p. 279). The dead people buried in Plum Grove Cemetery are a "thousand seeds" of which "never one will sprout" (p. 234).

The poet has many ways of "imaging" life. It is "a stream flowing toward some sea" (p. 107). It is also the season of a flower from blossom to decay (p. 16). At other times it is a furrow made by a plow (p. 18), and a young man is "an oak bud bursting into bloom" (p. 268). Equally impressive are images of death and the dead person. In addition to those listed above, there is the crushed petal (p. 270), the drawing of a curtain (p. 37), a trip down the hill, and the coming of autumn (p. 346). Death may also be symbolized by the falling of a leaf or a journey west.

Although the rhetorical figure seems completely natural to Stuart, critics appear to be at odds about the importance of symbolism in his work. Wade Hall, for one, recognizes the significance of metaphor:

It is probably in his reproduction of the natural metaphors of folk speech that Stuart achieves his greatest linguistic success. The use of metaphorical language allows the speaker to be more vivid and earthy than the educated person whose speech is filled with a plethora of adjectives and adverbs derived from Latin and Greek.[2]

While hailing Stuart's metaphors as linguistically successful, Hall is reluctant to find much value in the poet's symbolism:

In Stuart's books the earth is the earth is the earth. He occasionally uses nature for symbols, but he prefers to let a river be a river and a tree a tree. His meanings are generally as direct and as basic as the earth itself. And the earth is rather profound. Symbol-hunting pedants could conclude that "grass" in Stuart's fiction and poetry is as much a symbol of life or immortality—or whatever—as it is in Whitman's poetry. Truly it is. But Stuart's grass is first and foremost grass. After all, symbolic grass does not grow in the ground of W-Hollow and green in the spring.[3]

Even though his observations are generally sound, Hall is wrong in his assessment of symbolism. The error in his thinking is obvious. He sees metaphor as being inherent in language and refers to a "reproduction of the natural metaphors of folk speech." At the same time, he does not see that the symbol is also inherent in language.

Concerning metaphor, Philip Wheelwright says that the test lies in the quality of what he calls semantic transformation—that is, "the psychic depth at which the things of the world, whether actual or fancied, are transmuted by the cool heat of the imagination."[4] According to Wheelwright, there are two kinds of semantic movement in metaphor. The first he calls epiphoric, in which a similarity is

---

2. *The Truth Is Funny: A Study of Jesse Stuart's Humor* (Terre Haute, Indiana, 1970), p. 5.
3. *Ibid.*, p. 36.
4. *Metaphor and Reality* (Bloomington, Indiana, 1962), p. 71.

expressed between something relatively well known, or concretely known, and something which is not well known; and the second is diaphoric, in which semantic movement through "certain particulars of experience" produce new meaning by juxtaposition. Wheelwright cites Northrop Frye, who contends that metaphor is simple juxtaposition, and Ezra Pound, who, relying on the Chinese ideogram as illustrative, produces a complex image by throwing a group of elements together without predication. What is gained in diaphor, says Wheelwright, is that "new qualities and new meanings can emerge, simply come into being, out of some hitherto ungrouped combination of elements."[5] Metaphor at its best, as is frequently the case in Stuart's poetry, is both epiphoric and diaphoric at the same time.

In contrast to metaphor, a symbol is stable and repeatable. Wheelwright's definition is simple and clear: "A symbol, in general, is a relatively stable and repeatable element of perceptual experience, standing for some larger meaning or set of meanings which cannot be given, or not fully given, in perceptual experience itself."[6] An image must be capable of undergoing recurrence in order to function symbolically. Consequently, when a symbol is successfully used in a poem it has already acquired its status through previous expression, and comes "into the new poem equipped with a set of associations that will be largely intelligible to the literate reader."[7] In short, a literary symbol must have a literary background and must possess a potential of allusive reference. As far as distribution is concerned, a symbol may be confined to a particular poem, may be repeated and developed throughout the work of a particular poet, or may be passed on from poet to poet. It may have significance for those who belong to a particular religion, or to a particular culture. Also, a symbol may be archetypal. That is, it may have a "fairly similar significance for all or a large portion of mankind, independently of

---

5. *Ibid.*, p. 85.
6. *Ibid.*, p. 92.
7. *Ibid.*, p. 97.

borrowing and historical influences."[8]

Within the parameters proposed by Wheelwright, Mary Washington Clarke is more accurate than Hall in her assessment of Stuart's symbolism:

> Seeing into the life of things in W-Hollow has given Stuart a voice to speak of the universal experience. Metaphors and symbols are almost surely best when they are least private and arbitrary. *Trees of Heaven* [an early novel] is such a natural metaphor for Stuart's theme. The earth, the snakes and lizards, the whispering wind and grass, the changing seasons are inevitable symbols in the poems of *Album of Destiny*. *Year of My Rebirth* is the view from Stuart's window in W-Hollow, a wider view than most of us ever see, expressing his love of earth and sky and all living things.[9]

Two phrases stand out above all others: "inevitable symbols" and "the universal experience." The first implies an observation that Wade Hall never seems to question, and that is that the symbols are as inevitable as the language which expresses them. Also implied is that the "inevitable symbols" are the ones referred to as "least private and arbitrary." In other words, successful symbols come naturally and harmoniously from the poet's use of language; they are not contrived. The second phrase, which is directly related to the first, seems to indicate that "the universal experience" is a consequence or concomitant of the "inevitable symbols." Ruel Foster refers to the process as "a kind of unconscious welling up,"[10] and in doing so hits upon the key issue—that of consciousness. Conscious symbolism, that which is fabricated, internalizes and becomes personal. Unconscious symbolism, by virtue of its being unconscious, externalizes and becomes impersonal. In light of this fact, and in light of Stuart's conscious attempt to use symbols in *Album of Destiny*, one wonders why Clarke

---

8. *Ibid.*, p. 99.
9. *Jesse Stuart's Kentucky* (New York, 1968), p. 220.
10. *Jesse Stuart* (New York, 1968), p. 153.

located the "inevitable symbols" there.

As indicated earlier, the poet says that he deliberately planned the symbols in his collection. And Everetta Love Blair notes his disappointment concerning how they were received:

> Stuart was particularly disappointed that none of the critics mentioned the symbolism woven throughout this work, with the black snake representing Good and the copperhead Evil.[11]

Given Blair's explanation about the blacksnake and the copperhead, one can readily see why such attempts at symbolism fail. Granted, good and evil are universal. But snakes in general, depending on the part of the world one is in, may be good, evil, good and evil, good or evil. Snakes in particular—the common blacksnake and the copperhead—are not universal. Therefore, to let the blacksnake represent good and the copperhead evil is meaningless in those parts of the world where no such snakes exist.

In looking at the entire Stuart canon, one suspects that the contriving of symbols began earnestly in *Album of Destiny*, and for two closely related reasons. Most obvious is that the collection was intended to overcome his declining reputation as poet. But that *Man with a Bull-Tongue Plow* (1934) was so frequently referred to by reviewers as "merely regional" is probably a more important one. Everyone who has written extensively about Jesse Stuart—Ramey, Leavell, Foster, Hall, Clarke, Blair, and Pennington—has had to grapple with the problem of regionalism in his writing. About it the poet himself has said: "It hurts you, whatever it is."[12] Though all of the scholars named above concur in the idea that his writing is more than "merely regional," only Lee Pennington has launched a major effort to settle the matter.

---

11. *Jesse Stuart: His Life and Works* (Columbia, South Carolina, 1967), p. 48. The poet's fascination with snakes is perhaps best demonstrated in *Dawn of Remembered Spring* (New York, 1972).
12. Interview, taped at W-Hollow, May 31, 1971.

Unfortunately, Pennington's study of symbolism begins on a defensive note: "Jesse Stuart has been called a regionalist too long."[13] He qualifies by explaining that the poet is not a regionalist in the disparaging sense of the term, only in the finer or literary sense. There is a basic set of symbols, he espouses, which begins in *Harvest of Youth* and continues throughout all of the work, though he limits his study to the first book of poems and the novels. He interprets the work in terms of the old but well-known struggle between forces of light and forces of darkness. The moon, the clouds, the sun, and the sea are important symbols in the struggle. He also identifies what he refers to as a symbolic woman and a symbolic youth, maintaining that the latter is the most important of all the symbols: "Youth is immediately the symbol of a rebirth which has already taken place. It is an embodiment of the present, a part of the past, and the only link to the future."[14] In other words, he sees the ritual pattern of life-death-resurrection coming from antiquity as adequate for interpreting the symbols. After all, he argues, Stuart's theme is that of a dying culture—the old way of life that once existed in Appalachia.

In the conclusion to his book, Pennington asserts once again that the ultimate appeal of the symbols is universal:

> Stuart selected the dark hills and the people of the dark hills because the hills are the home of the people of darkness, and these sons and daughters of darkness are symbols for a far greater concept concerning the nature of man. The people, like the concept of man in the Twentieth Century, are lost, lonely and forgotten. Yet, from the dark hills and the people of darkness can come a world of light. Whether Stuart believes the world of light will come we can only guess; that he believes it is possible we know. He has spent a lifetime saying it is possible.[15]

---

13. *The Dark Hills of Jesse Stuart* (Cincinnati, 1967), p. i.
14. *Ibid.*, p. 28.
15. *Ibid.*, p. 153.

The writer of such a commentary is convincing when, momentarily, he forgets to be defensive—when he forgets all about good regionalism and bad regionalism. (Because of the importance of the topic of regionalism to Stuart's success as a poet, and the impossibility of doing the topic justice here, it will be discussed in more detail in Chapter 8.) He is also convincing when he discusses symbolism in general in place of the symbol in particular. But he is least impressive when he concocts an explanation, which he frequently does, that the symbols are consciously planned and executed. He would be even more acceptable if he could believe that the best symbols are those which call the least attention to themselves—that symbols, like metaphors, similes, and other rhetorical devices, exist solely for the purpose of imaging life, and that their collective success is the only true measure of their value.

Whether studying symbolism or not, one must bear in mind that Jesse Stuart's pictures are scenes, a composite of which make up his pastoral world of W-Hollow. The following lines contain one of the few instances in which he takes the reader inside a house or any other building:

> And cozily we sat by our fireside
> And ate of corn and supped of berry-wine;
> We sat and let the snow-world drift outside;
> We sat and watched through frosted window panes
> The snow flakes drifting through green tops of pines.
>
> (p. 6)

The view is a miniature of Whittier's "Snowbound," and possesses something of the nostalgia of that poem. Equally rare as his indoor scenes are his attempts to capture the facial and physical features of his characters. Portraits of people are either missing or are greatly exaggerated in *Man with a Bull-Tongue Plow*. About as close as he ever comes to painting such a portrait is represented in this attempt by an old mountaineer to describe God:

> I wot my God Almighty smoked a pipe,
> And with his bony fingers combed and wiped

The backer ashes from his long white beard.
God Almighty was a little man, I heerd—
                                    (p. 55)

The lines are delightful because of the mountain dialect, and because of the details—bony fingers, tobacco ashes, and white beard—which could be used in describing the mountaineer himself. God is humanized in terms of the man's own existence.

Stuart paints best when he is looking at natural things. Such pictures as the one of birds flying south (p. 10) and the one of pansies growing among chips of cow-dung (p. 111) are impressive because of their sensuous detail. They are compact and concentrated. The following sonnet, by contrast, paints more comprehensively:

The multi-colored leaves are dying now,
Some hang like golden jewels to the bough,
And with the wind the pretty leaves go flying,
Over fields empty and forgotten now.
And in the wind the bare tree-tops are sighing,
Rabbits have found new drifts for sleeping now
Where briars have caught the leaves
        and held them down.
When there is not room in the stack and mow,
And cattle bed on dead leaves drifted down
In briars—And overhead day-drifting skies
Are filled with flying leaves and wild-bird cries.
The birds at night sleep in the shocks of fodder
On rugged hills beside the Sandy water.
                                    (p. 11)

The poet attempts to unify details with the leaf, or with leaves, but whether they all stay on the canvas is questionable. They likely do not. He might have succeeded had he started with the cattle bedded on the ground and then proceeded to paint around them.

The sonnet form, for a painter-poet, has distinct advantages. For the narrator of incidents, as Stuart learned even before *Man with a Bull-Tongue Plow,* the sonnet is suitable for purposes of compression, limiting greatly the number of details in any one incident. The incident recounted, in that collection, often becomes the scene painted, and it was the recognition of this as a possibility that brought about his increased emphasis on scene-painting. The sonnet, viewed in this way, became a field to be filled, and although it did not allow him to abandon words and turn to the pure poetry found only in the objects of nature, it did allow him to think and to construct with things rather than with words foremost in mind. The problems for one who paints with words are numerous. Line, balance, and proportion must remain highly suggestive rather than controlled. And for Stuart, this proved to be beneficial. He tried to paint by suggestion, as Whitman had done—to fall back on Emerson's idea that each word could be a poem. By juxtaposing his words, he found that he could paint. He discovered that a list of words could signify objects or things, and that by selecting and arranging his words in sequence, he could exercise considerable control over his painting.

The poet compiles many catalogues in *Man with a Bull-Tongue Plow.* He fills sonnet after sonnet with things that he hates, loves, sees, hears, smells, wants or does not want. One sequence on leave-taking alone contains eleven sonnets in which he simply names things, bringing his W-Hollow milieu into existence (pp. 339-344). He categorizes people who are buried in Plum Grove Cemetery:

> Here sleep the good and bad and rich and poor,
> The sinister, wife, the maid, the wretch and whore;
> The soldier, farmer, merchant and the thief;
>
> (p. 271)

Interestingly enough, titles on grave markers differ:

> Some have grave markers giving their brief past;
> Telling their titles such as husbands, wives,

> Sisters, uncles, aunts, and brothers, mothers,
> Soldiers and infant sons and infant daughters.
>
> (p. 236)

There are other groupings of these Plum Grove dead, and each time the titles change to fit the immediate context.

The catalogues often contain highly sensuous details, as in this one of things seen:

> I see the blood of autumn in the wind,
> The wine-red blood of apple tree and peach;
> The yellow blood of poplar tree and beech;
> I see the blood of autumn drifting in
> The fence rows and the stools of green briar thickets;
> I see trees still a-bleeding down red drops;
> Black-oak, birch, elm, black gum; from their tall tops
> The blood drips like fresh water from old spickets.
>
> (p. 217)

As the first and last lines indicate, such a method does not exclude using figures of speech, but rather may encourage it, depending somewhat upon the purpose. The list itself may consist of practical things like tools:

> And we must gather now the rakes and plows,
> And mattocks, spades, pitchforks, and garden hoes,
> Stack them away just as the summer goes; (p. 184)

Or it may consist of different kinds of one thing, such as leaves:

> The sourwood leaves hang clustered red as blood,
> The dogwood leaves are falling to the ground,
> The poplar leaves drift in a windy flood,
> From their tall tops drift slowly to the ground.
>
> (p. 183)

He sometimes uses the sonnet to narrate an incident and thereby paint a picture. In this one, for instance, Elizabeth's coming late is an appropriate occasion for flowers:

You came too late to see us, my Elizabeth,
Wild roses by the rocks have lost their bloom;
And their soft petals now have curled beneath
The barren stems to meet a dead-leaf doom.
You came too late to see the blood-root in
White blooms along the worm rail fence corners;
Too late to see wild yuccas in the wind—
You came too late to see wild lady's-fingers,
But you are here to see the wild larkspur;
Blue beggar lice, and wild wind-loved jonquils.
You have come to my Kentucky where
The goldenrod are turning on the hills.
Susans are yellow as a brush-pile flame;
You have come late, but I am glad you came.
                                        (p. 166)

In addition to what it says, the poem is highly suggestive
with implications of Elizabeth's coming late found in the
flowers.

The following is one of the sonnets of leave-taking. In
what appears to be a random collection of objects, the poet
paints his pastoral world:

Farewell to birds a-roosting in the fodder;
Farewell to naked hills with white-rock seams,
To black leaves drifting on the slushy water;
Farewell to all my native hills and streams—
The dark hills there against the threatening skies;
And cold white leghorn chickens in dark trees;
The trains of crows and their soft searching cries,
Farewell to all and cold snakes under leaves;
Farewell to ragweed fields where rabbits hide
And high rock cliffs where foxes make their dens;
Farewell to straw-pens where the quails abide;
Farewell to smoke from huts of hunting men;
Farewell to winter winds that make their moan;
Farewell to families by their warm hearthstone.
                                        (p. 189)

Surely, such a poem indicates that Stuart is a Namer, but he is more than that. For each object he also finds a characteristic feature, which leads to a necessary relationship. The relationship, in turn, not only gets more objects into the picture but also gives them an appropriate context: "crows" roost in "fodder," "hills" have "white-rock seams," and "leaves" drift on "water." Things named are detailed more succinctly by the word in the position of the adjective. The "hills" are "naked," the "leaves" are "black," the "water" is "slushy," the "skies" are "threatening," and the crows have "cries" that are "soft" and "searching." Such details have significant sensuous appeal and impose definite limitations and restrictions upon the reader. Smoke, for example, is very general, but smoke "from the huts of hunting men," in contrast to smoke from the smokestacks of steel mills and iron foundries, is what one would expect in a pastoral world. Through naming the objects, relating the objects, and qualifying the relationships in *Man with a Bull-Tongue Plow,* Stuart paints the pictures that hang in his W-Hollow gallery.

In assessing imagery in *Album of Destiny* one needs to look at what Stuart has said about the book as well as what he has done in it. When he wrote it, he was most certainly thinking of the collection as a picture-gallery containing five groups of paintings: "This was the idea for my book. Take these people whose photographs had been made in the springtime of their lives and write portraits of them in verse."[16] He planned four portraits of them, he explains, to show what happened to them as the years passed. The idea, then, was that there would be more than one album or picture-gallery. There were to be four albums of pictures of the same people and a final one devoted to their children. When his portraits were completed, they would represent the stages of man's life, the seasons of the year, and through representing the children in an album of their own he would

16. "Why I Think *Album* Is My Best," *Prairie Schooner* 30 (1956), 32.

complete the ancient life-death-resurrection pattern. As Stuart aptly puts it, each additional album after the first was to show "what happened to them." He wanted to get away from painting still lifes and to produce in their stead a cinematic effect which would correspond to the panoramic quality that he had learned how to produce in the individual poem by listing or cataloguing physical details. *Album of Destiny*, as he planned it, would be a "moving picture" in which the reader saw one generation grow up and finally die off, much in the way that a leaf or flower does. But the picture would not stop there. It was to have no end, as does the film at a cinema. It would simply start all over again in a "resurrected spring."[17]

Stuart apparently believed that he could accomplish what he planned. He shifted the voice, replacing that of the poet with those of the fifty characters in the portraits, who talk to and about each other. Furthermore, the running commentary which is so much before the reader in *Man with a Bull-Tongue Plow* all but disappears in *Album of Destiny*, suggesting a willingness to let the art stand on its own. What commentary there is belongs to the characters. Worth Sutton, in one instance, says to his brother Randall:

My songs come from the stubble and the flower;
They come from cornfield dirt and fighting blood.
My songs come from the thrush note and the shower,
From the green ragweed blood in solitude.
These are American songs, for in my moods
I sing American from American blood,
With words that drip with blue Kentucky mud.[18]

In the next sonnet Araminta Sutton replies:

---

17. *Ibid.*, p. 33.
18. AD, p. 213. There is no point in indicating titles for the poems in *Album of Destiny* (New York, 1944). Titles are captions that give directions, something like the directions that one would expect in a play script. The caption for this poem, for example, is "Worth to Randall," and for the next one it is "Araminta to Worth."

Sing out, wild heart! Sing in your windy mood,
Sing to the playful wind, sing your gay song,
Sing out, wild blood, sing songs of your wild blood;
Sing out, sing gay, sing, sing, go sing your song.
This is your life, this is your native land;
These are your hills, your rivers, and your bottoms.
Sing out your songs, your people, and your land,
Through winters, springs, the summers and the autumns.
Sing, sing, of ox carts, wagon wheels, and plows,
Sing of the little world where you belong,
The round-log shacks, cornfields, mules, and spotted cows.
Sing, poet, sing, sing, sing wildly wild your song.
Remember song was in you from beginning,
Back in your sires in drinking and in sinning.
                                        (p. 213)

References such as these have no weight as commentary on
the poet's art. Instead, they are musical interludes, celebra-
tions in which the significance of song lies in the activity of
singing in much the same way that the value of life lies in the
activity of living. A similar situation is found in the activity
of the dance:

On with the dance though time be slivered glass!
On with the dance until the break of day!
On with the dance before we mortals pass!
                                        (p. 104)

Here the dance is symbolic of life, and the worthwhileness of
either is simply that of being in it.

Worth Sutton's "words that drip with blue Kentucky
mud" are, as he says, the words that belong to the songs of an
old agricultural or frontier America—a frontier America ar-
rested in Stuart's W-Hollow. Araminta and Worth both know
the objects belonging to that frontier world. It is pastoral,
and so much so that Stuart tries to capture it in one symbolic
portrait:

For Volgares Welch

Young shepherd with your sheep in tumbled hills,
Whistle your tunes soft as the spring winds cry
Among pine fingers, over April rills
Where wild white-breasted birds go winging by
With sedgegrass straws to build in stools of briars.
Shepherd of tumbled hills, your cloud-white flock
Nipping the thin grass by the rusted wires
And climbing high upon the jagged rock
To whet away the hoofs they do not need . . .
Blow winds of April scented with percoon
And rustle sourwood leaves of purplish-red
And cool the flock, for night does not come soon.
Whistle your tunes, young Shepherd, to your flock
In tumbled hills before you have to keep
Vigil for lambs and ewes from dog and fox
Corraled on the highest peak in quiet sleep.

                                        (p. 244)

Using the shepherd and his sheep, conventions of the ancient pastoral, the poet paints in miniature a telling portrait of his *Album of Destiny*.

Because the poet uses fifty voices, and frequently in a familial situation, any sequence of sonnets may result in a forum or dialogue. The exchange between Worth and Araminta Sutton is typical. In some instances, the range of the dialogue is more restricted:

Millie Seymore Frainwood and Her Son

Son: Mother, you said my Daddy would be home
         Before the yard was green with grass again.
         The yard is green, why hasn't Daddy come?
         And when he comes, will Daddy ride the train?
Mother: My Son, your Daddy is somewhere at sea
         And he'll be home soon as the war is won.
Son: Then Daddy will come home to you and me!
Mother: Yes, yes, your Daddy will be home, my Son.

Son: And when he comes I want to meet the train,
          Show him my dog, my marbles and my gun!
Mother: When he comes home we'll go to meet his train;
          Your Daddy will be proud of you, his Son!
Voice: Mother, you know your husband won't be home,
          Only four Frainwoods fight for Liberty:
          Your son will wait and wait for him
          to come . . .
          Two Frainwoods fell on land, one lost at sea!

                                     (p. 250)

The sonnet is interesting because it consciously employs techniques of the dramatist, including that of labelling the change in speakers. Although it is overly sentimental and not convincing as poetry, it successfully illustrates the importance of dialogue—the importance of relating a situation through the voices of the people who are in it. Spectacle seems less important than it does in the dialogue of the Suttons, although character, situation, and spectacle are all three essential to the playwright.

In *Album of Destiny,* as in *Man with a Bull-Tongue Plow,* Stuart often names the sense and then enumerates things loved, hated, seen, heard, smelled, and touched. Lying in bed and listening to sounds that come from outside, Luster Stark hears the "rattle in the green leaves' throats" (p. 41), and Wincie Sutton comments to Worth:

> The monotone of rain you love to hear,
> Drops beat the dirt like drums far in the night.
> You love to put your hands on the green tree
> And feel the ooze of water on the bark.
>
>   (p. 214)

The hand feeling the "ooze of water" on the bark of the "green tree" is powerful in its direct sensuous appeal. John Sutton labels the things that he loves to smell, again identifying the poet as Namer.[19] In one poem the catalogue includes goldenrod, stagnant water, mushrooms, buttercups, needle-and-the-thread, sassafras, vines, possum grapes, wild honey-suckle winds, chigger-daisies, wilted corn, and rotten apples (p. 78).

Such an immersion of the reader's senses should allow him to stand at a distance and view himself among—while examining—the objects. That would be to escape the words, to get beyond language and vicarious experience, and to the point of experiencing the world of physical objects firsthand. In order to make the objects more accessible, the poet has his characters view each other among them, and talk to each other as though they are not only there, but as though they could be nowhere else. For example, John Sutton sees his wife Kathaleen as an extension of the objects around her: "You, lithe, blue-eyed with golden wheat-straw hair, / You with your fine-curved lips and leaf-tan face" (p. 79). With his image of the path, Jack Porter illustrates the problem that exists for Stuart the poet: "The path that leads me to my highland home / Has left its twisted image on my brain" (p. 150). The world of the real path is a hard physical one. That of the image on the brain is a world apart. Somewhere between the two there must exist a bridge, and that is language.

The symbol or word is not the same as the thing symbolized. As his many catalogues illustrate, the poet has examined carefully the possibilities and the limitations of symbolism. Emerson's idea of the word as emblem is illustrated in the following sonnet by one of his characters who is somewhere in the South Pacific:

---

19. The section of poems entitled "Songs of the Summer Sun" constitutes one long list of names of things found in rural Kentucky. This portion of *Album of Destiny* alone is convincing evidence of the extent to which Stuart had come to think of himself as the Namer and Sayer of words. Further, it is also evidence of the extent to which he had come to rely on panoramic imagery, that is, in simply naming the objects and thereby evoking sensuous response, as does Walt Whitman.

Delmar Landgraves

These are the symbols of the land I love:
Log cabins on high banks of yellow clay,
A stream of water threading through a cove,
Tobacco barn's slow sagging to decay;
An apple orchard where the rabbits hide
In greenbriar clusters in the unkept balk,
A frontyard paling gate that can't swing wide,
Gnarled shade trees where the old folks sit and talk.
These are the scenes embedded in my brain:
The cabin's chimney made of cornfield rocks,
The sunflowers reaching to the windowpane,
The garden palings rowed with hollyhocks.
These are the symbols of the land that's mine,
Encircled by hills reaching for the sun,
And friendly fingers of the cliff-grown pine
That swish clean wind where mountain waters run.

(p. 227)

It is likely unfair to talk about such a poem as "Delmar Landgraves" without considering all of it, including versification. In the first place, the poet is obviously composing by line. All except two lines are end-stopped, and the reason is that the line is a unit containing a single image.[20] In each of the two exceptions the image is completed in the second line. As the basic unit of composition in the poem, the line not only limits or defines the image, but as the end-stops indicate, it is both a thought unit and a rhythmic unit. The result is that the images are clearly defined by time. They correspond to the line as a unit of composition, and are completed within it. Thus the panoramic effect of the imagery is enhanced.

In *Album of Destiny,* as in *Man with a Bull-Tongue Plow,* Stuart used as many means as he could to get his pictures before the reader. The remarkable thing is that he still did not attempt to picture the faces of any of his characters. A

20. Also excepted are lines 1, 9, and 13. Breaking the sixteen-line sonnet into an octet and two quatrains, these group the images and reiterate an expression that has the effect of a refrain.

companion-piece to the mountaineer's description of God in *Man with a Bull-Tongue Plow,* Jackie Sizemore's description of the devil is about as close as he came:

> As sure as God, I know I seen the Devil
> A-going up the road, and on his back
> He carried a pitchfork, pick, longhandled shovel,
> A coffee pot and ragged coffee-sack.
>
> (p. 100)

The poet seems incapable of seeing people as people. As in Jim Higgins' description of Murt Higgins, the person being painted gets lost:

> She was five ten with eyes of dark midnight
> With high cheekbones and hair black as charcoal;
> Her teeth were white as March percoon is white,
> Her fingers tapering limbs of marigold.
>
> (p. 153)

Descriptions in his fiction are quite similar, as is this attempt to describe Deutsia Huntoon, a young Melungeon woman:

> Her hair was as golden as a poplar leaf ripened by early October's sun. It fell loosely down her back almost to her knees. I'd never seen hair that long and as October-poplar-leaf-golden as hers. She looked at me with soft blue eyes shaded by heavy lashes. Her eyes were blue as the petals of mountain violets. Her sun-tanned face had the smoothness and color of a ripe-hickory-nut stripped of its shell. She was tall and slender, straight as a sapling, with slim ankles and shapely nut-brown legs.[21]

The opening paragraph of the novel for which he is best known also contains such a description:

> Grandpa's brogan shoes made a noise like whettin two rocks together as he shuffled them back and forth on the witherin school-yard grass. I stood beside Grandpa and

---

21. *Daughter of the Legend* (New York, 1965), p. 3.

watched him work his feet in his crumple-toed brogan shoes while the hot July wind played with Grandpa's white beard. The wind lifted Grandpa's white corn-silk beard up and down but it couldn't tear it away from his face. His beard grew to his pale face for I could see it growing there when the wind lifted it up and down. I stood beside Grandpa and looked up and down his tall body; he looked as tall as a tree to me. But Grandpa didn't look as straight as a young tree. He was bent like an old tree weighted down with branches.[22]

On the next page of the same book he tries to describe a face:

Uncle Mott's face had lost its sun-browned color. His face was almost as white as the milkweed furze that I've tried to catch on the meader. But the wind lifted it like it lifted Grandpa's beard—it lifted it higher and higher and I ran under it and couldn't reach it. Uncle Mott's face was nearly that white. I'd say it was more the color of a yellow clay road when it dries out in the spring. His face had the same color of dried clay where the sun has left big cracks in it.[23]

Descriptions in his stories closely resemble those in the poems and the novels. Genre appears to make little or no difference. "Love in the Spring," which is representative, contains a description of Effie Long, a young woman who attends a spring baptizing:

She was prettier than a speckled pup. Honest I never saw anything like her. Eyes that just looked at you and melted like yellow butter on hot corn bread—blue kind of eyes—and a face that was smooth as silk and cheeks the color of the peeling on a roman beauty apple in September. Her hair was the color of golden corn silks in August hanging from the shooting corn.[24]

---

22. *Taps for Private Tussie* (New York, 1943), p. 9.
23. *Ibid.*, p. 10.
24. *Come Gentle Spring* (New York, 1969), p. 56.

The same device, that of describing the individual in terms of the objects surrounding him, is used in "Yoked for Life":

> Uncle Jeff was a big man. He weighed three hundred seven pounds. He was six feet two, and there were no bulges on his powerful body. He was a muscular man with arms as big as small fence posts, legs at the calves as big as gate posts, and hands as big as shovels.[25]

This method is consistent throughout the poetry and the fiction, and the reason for it lies within Stuart's philosophy of Being. Pat Hennessey sees the explanation in the stem of an apple, and explains the apple tree as "Maker of a dream":

> An apple coming through such slender stem!
> And when my mother came, I stood beside her.
> She was the tree and I was fruit born of her.
> (p. 93)

As Whitman had done before him, Stuart hurled his ego into the objects he found in nature and came to identify his ego with the creative processes that he found there. The mysterious creation of an apple through such a slender stem is appropriately symbolic of the mystery of all creation. Woman, too, he believes, is "builder of a dream." Significantly, the mystery does not belong to men, for they cannot explain it. Both the mystery and the ego of the poet become wild and primitive, as indicated in this poem from *Man with a Bull-Tongue Plow:*

> The rain falls from the slack-pile heavens to
> An earth that's covered with dead grass and leaves.
> The rain falls down among the barren trees.
> The lightnings scar the heavens—flashes through
> Dark pages of the earth—the grass blades quiver,
> And strong trees bend to reckless elements.
> Ah, I would love to say: Storm rage forever!
> I love to see your lightning cut the sky!

---

25. *My Land Has a Voice* (New York, 1966), p. 15.

I'd love to see your naked woods washed clean!
I love to hear your wind and waters cry!
I love that cool incessant monotone;
This would make me go wild and live alone!
The passionate surging of the elements!
Surgings like passions of primitive men!

(p. 156)

Here, also, the poet composes by line, and the last three make clear what there is in the raging storm that attracts him. In Freudian terms the id, which is primitive and wild, is held in check or civilized through some mysterious interaction with the ego and the superego. In the meantime the poet sees himself as belonging there in the "passionate surging of the elements." The passions of the elements are like those of primitive men, we are told. They are the passions of Stuart's ancestors—those "tall figures of the earth" who fought back the wilderness.

A quick glance at line five opens up many new possibilities for exploration. Not only is the ego of the poet to be identified with the storm, but so is his poetry. The earth is a book, and for Stuart poetry exists in whatever is alive to the senses—beyond words. In the "passionate surging" of the storm one finds the image. It is there that the poet, in the process of discovering himself among the objects, catches a fleeting glimpse of what he really is. After the storm, there remains only the "image on the album of the brain." From that image the poet creates his own storm, one that is to be experienced vicariously by others. To say that the poet's storm is the storm in nature would be misleading. As Stuart knows, a lion in the cage is not the same as a lion in the jungle.

8

The Constant Agrarian: Some Tentative Conclusions

There remain a number of vital questions which need to be answered concerning Jesse Stuart's present position in American letters. There are questions about his career as a chronicler, and about what has been gained through that approach. There are very important questions about his being a regional writer, a popular writer, and about his apparent disregard for the direction that American art has taken. Admittedly, the last issue may not be a matter of disregard, for art takes the direction of a culture, and since the 1930s Stuart has been honestly and openly opposed to the direction that American culture has taken. In short, he must be assessed in terms of his objections to what has happened to American culture and to the American sensibility. They are real issues, the concerns about which he has been writing consistently, in spite of the fact that his critics have devoted neither the time nor the effort to examine his writings for a controlling vision. Heretofore Jesse Stuart has been one of the most poorly evaluated and most misunderstood writers in America, but that fact in no way dismisses his faults. He has them, and they deserve to be examined along with the nature and gravity of the misunderstanding.

When John Bird called Stuart an anachronism in his

essay for *Saturday Evening Post* in 1959,[1] he may not have
fully understood or appreciated the importance of what he
was saying. He could see the causes were determined by time
and place—happy circumstances—but the time and the place
Bird identified are too restricting. Being born in Eastern Ken-
tucky in 1907 did not give Stuart his vision as a writer, as
important as those conditions were. Nor is Lee Pennington's
argument that Stuart's vision is that of a dying culture en-
tirely satisfactory.[2] Like Bird, Pennington gives too much
credence to Appalachia, and too little to the culture upper-
most in Stuart's mind. Pennington is also like Bird in that he
completely ignores the real source of Stuart's vision, although
he should have at least suspected it upon reading the last sec-
tion of poems in *Man with a Bull-Tongue Plow.*

Spending the academic year of 1931-1932 at Vanderbilt
University was the most important single event in shaping
Jesse Stuart's vision as a thinker and writer, and the fact that
Donald Davidson told the young poet to go home and write
about his own hill country is merely symptomatic of what
would take shape as a pervasive and wide-ranging influence.
In 1972 McGraw-Hill reprinted *Beyond Dark Hills*, and in the
Foreword, written for the new edition, Stuart writes:

> When I was an undergraduate student at Lincoln Memo-
> rial University, Harrogate, Tennessee, I read books by
> writers who called themselves the Fugitives of Vander-
> bilt University, Nashville, Tennessee. Here were writers
> who had joined together in an organization. Part or all
> were in the Agrarian Movement—"pro" back to the farms
> and "anti" industrialization of the South. Being a farmer
> then, as I am still, all of this was attractive to me. . . . I
> had always had in mind going to Vanderbilt University,
> where teachers wrote books and farmed. I wanted to be

---

1. See Chapter 1. For Bird's remark see *Saturday Evening Post* 232
(July 25, 1959), 79.
2. See *The Dark Hills of Jesse Stuart* (Cincinnati, 1967), pp. 5-35 in
particular.

part of this group. Vanderbilt was my dream school. It had to be Vanderbilt.[3]

The first number of *The Fugitive* was published in Nashville in 1922 and the last in 1925, which was six years before Stuart went to Vanderbilt. The Fugitives disbanded upon publication of *Fugitives: An Anthology of Verse* in 1928, but Louise Cowan contends that their influence was far-reaching: "The Nashville poets who published the little magazine *The Fugitive* during the early half of the 1920's have the distinction of being the inaugurators of the Southern literary renaissance."[4] Cowan singles out from others in the group Ransom, Davidson, Tate, and Warren as the most germinal and articulate. They also played major roles in the Agrarian Movement, and it is not entirely without justification, says Cowan, that the general literary public has tended to merge the two movements. Among the four writers there were growing ideological differences which would manifest themselves in the form of a controversy over T. S. Eliot's poem *The Waste Land*. In 1922 Ransom unfavorably reviewed Eliot's poem and Tate rose to defend Eliot. The incident enhanced what had already developed in the group as an acute awareness of the age that saw Ransom and Tate moving farther and farther apart. Ransom would increasingly resist modernism, defending the old English tradition of meter and rhyme. In turn, Tate would accelerate his defense of the new school of Symbolists.

It is generally conceded that *The Waste Land* is an indictment of Western civilization, and that the inhabitants of the wasted land are sterile and spiritually dead. Tate's "Ode to the Confederate Dead" is also a Symbolist poem in which conditions are those of a wasteland:

> The shut gate and the decomposing wall:
> The gentle serpent, green in the mulberry bush,

---

3. See Stuart's Foreword in *Beyond Dark Hills* (New York, 1972), pp. xi-xii. Also see his autobiographical essay "Three Teachers and a Book," *Pages* (Detroit, 1976), pp. 90-103.
4. *The Fugitive Group: A Literary History* (Baton Rouge, Louisiana, 1959), p. xv.

Riots with his tongue through the hush—
Sentinel of the grave who counts us all![5]

Like Eliot, Tate sees man caught in the present, honoring and glorifying a past in which he cannot live. What Jesse Stuart acquired from the Fugitives is an overwhelming consciousness of the conditions of a dying American culture in general and of a Southern culture in particular.

The Fugitives shared their awareness of cultural decadence in the South with William Faulkner, and they placed much of the blame for those conditions on the old pre-Civil War ideal of Jeffersonian society. Nevertheless, the Agrarians came full circle and actually cultivated Jeffersonian idealism. Stuart is right about what the Agrarians stood for. *I'll Take My Stand* was published in 1930—a year before Stuart went to Vanderbilt—and the end of the very first paragraph in "Introduction: A Statement of Principles" makes clear the matter of intent: "All the articles bear in the same sense upon the book's title-subject: all tend to support a Southern way of life against what may be called the American or prevailing way; and all as much as agree that the best terms in which to represent the distinction are contained in the phrase, Agrarian *versus* Industrial."[6] One does not read very far before he has found the basic assumptions: that technology robs man of his dignity by removing him from his intimate relationship with the soil, that religion cannot be expected to flourish in an industrial society, that art cannot thrive under industrialism because there is a general decay of sensibility in an industrial state, that the social amenities suffer in an industrial state, and that philosophical humanism without practical humanism—questioning social and economic life—is rather shortsighted. Obviously the individual is of central importance, and that would be lost, so the Agrarians feared, in an industrial state.

The Agrarian Movement took place in the wake of a great

---

5. *Poems* (New York, 1960), p. 23.
6. Cited from the Harper Torchbook Edition (New York, 1962), p. xix.

depression; consequently Southern thinkers and writers blamed the depression on the evils of big city life and industrialism. In turn they went back and picked up the myth-building effort that had been launched before the Civil War, when artists had been instrumental in promoting sectional pride and patriotism. What resulted was what W. J. Cash, in *The Mind of the South*, calls "a sort of stage piece out of the eighteenth century."[7] What really happened, according to Cash, is that the splendor of the Old World, driven from England by Cromwell, found a new home in the American South. It was a way of life characterized by ideals of honor and nobility reminiscent of Faulkner's *verities* found in the Latin humanists. C. Hugh Holman, in "The View from the Regency-Hyatt: Southern Social Issues and the Outer World," admirably explains that the Agrarians chose the legend over the facts:

> And there is also a South which is a lost paradise of order and stability, of honor and a religious view of man. This South is a challenge, an ideal, and a star by which to steer, even though the mariners themselves admit that it really is a light never seen on land or sea. This is the South of the Vanderbilt Agrarians, a South which has proved to be a powerfully dynamic symbol of agrarian opposition to capitalistic industrialism. It has been magnificently celebrated in some of the best poetry and fiction of the region as a repository of the finest traditions of the old South.[8]

The Agrarian Movement was short-lived, and the Southern literary renascence died in the decade of the Forties.[9] There have been a few exceptions, but the greatest exception is the writing of Jesse Stuart. The Fugitive sense of the dec-

---

7. (New York, 1941), p. ix. For a convincing description see Cash's "Preview to Understanding," pp. vii-xi.
8. *Southern Fiction Today*, ed. George Core (Athens, Georgia, 1969), pp. 17-18.
9. See Walter Sullivan's "Southern Writers in the Modern World: Death by Melancholy," *Southern Review* 6 (1970), 907-919.

adence of the times and the Agrarian sense of the importance of place have been central to almost everything Stuart has written for the last forty-five years. He has remained on the farm, but more importantly he has written W-Hollow into his canon as "a lost paradise of order and stability." Stuart went home from Vanderbilt convinced that armchair Agrarianism was not enough; the style of his life and the style of his writing both attest to that fact.

No one in twentieth-century American literature has been more obsessed than Jesse Stuart with the significance of place as a source of identity—with the need for roots: "My country [Appalachia] has been my fountainhead, my source, my inspiration, my everything."[10] For literary purposes Robert Frost created a mythical country somewhere north of Boston, and William Faulkner created his famed Yoknapatawpha County. Stuart has done the same thing in Appalachia. The real Appalachia has changed drastically, but the one created by the poet for literary purposes has not changed. It is held in place by his own imagination, as a vehicle for promoting morality and thereby preserving a sense of dignity which he cannot find anywhere else. As he well knows, the dignity of man has been threatened in modern America, and the reasons, as far as he is concerned, are those once espoused by the Agrarians.

In Stuart's most recent novel, one finds nature being destroyed by technology:

> When we reached the top we stood on the divide and looked down. We could see well now, for darkness had left and lightness had come to the land, and I saw what I'd never seen in my life before. Two big giant machines would go up the slopes and come back down pushing trees out by the roots. If the helpless tree tried to stand, the big bulldozer would climb upon it and push and over it would go.[11]

---

10. *The Year of My Rebirth* (New York, 1956), pp. 264-265.
11. *The Land Beyond the River* (New York, 1973), p. 61.

The book's title is *The Land Beyond the River*, the land which is Ohio in this case, but it is also the land of Northern industrialism, the land of false prosperity. In his most recent autobiographical book, he writes of his feeling for the place called W-Hollow:

> Each time I come back [from traveling] I rediscover my home. The hills and valley of W-Hollow are mostly our land by deed. It is also the land we own in our hearts. We feel this is true of all the people who have ever lived in W-Hollow. Whether or not they held deed to an acre of this land, they loved and owned it in their hearts. . . . Here there is a reverence for life. A reverence for life must reach to all the world.[12]

When Stuart returned home from Vanderbilt, he wrote most of the poems for *Man with a Bull-Tongue Plow,* but he was also working on poems for a collection which has never been published. Entitled "Songs of a Mountain Plowman," those poems offered the greatest possible evidence of his preoccupation with Fugitive and Agrarian interests.[13] The poet tells us where we have gone wrong as a nation:

> Americans have lost their love for land.
> Men have grown far away from land and plows,
> The greenback dollars hold them in command.
> (p. 17)

Addressing stalwart pioneer mothers who bore a race of brave and courageous Americans, he continues to draw the lines that separate past and present:

> And now I speak to you to tell you this:
> Your daughters of today of dreamers here
> Fear too much for the pleasures they might miss
> From early spring to winter of their year.
> If they would come to be as you have been

---

12. *My World* (Lexington, Kentucky, 1975), pp. 2-3.
13. See Chapter 5. The numbers refer to pages in the typescript, which is in Stuart's possession in W-Hollow.

> And get the stalwart sons you dreamers got,
> Then we would have a different world of men.
> But many have turned whorish and forgot
> Not all of life is found in the blue wine glass,
> Not all good life is made by wasted blood.
> And as they mingle in this whirlpool mass
> And change from little mood to little mood,
> If they could get the sons you dreamers got
> To give our country strength, avoiding riot. (p. 6)

As an indictment of American culture in the Thirties, such lines leave little doubt concerning where the young poet stood. Enraged by the direction that American culture was taking in the Thirties—"America now going past. / This is the changing world" (p. 16)—he admonished youth to do something about it. His vision was clearly moral, and it has not changed. One can trace it throughout the poems from the Thirties to the present.[14]

In his refusal to accept modern American culture, and concomitantly the modern American sensibility, Jesse Stuart parts company with Walt Whitman. Although their beginnings as poets were remarkably similar, the directions they took account for the great success of one and the slight success of the other. Whitman, too, began as a very traditional poet. His early newspaper pieces—published in such places as *The Long Island Democrat, The Brooklyn Daily Eagle*, and *The Advertiser*—belonged to the early American tradition imported from Europe, the tradition that was so important to such poets as Bryant, Longfellow, and Whittier. As early as 1840 Whitman published "Young Grimes," which was an imitation of the meter, stanzaic form, and rhyme scheme of an older poem:

> When old Grimes died, he left a son—
> The graft of worthy stock;

---

14. I have actually done this in a paper entitled "Jesse Stuart's Poetry as Fugitive-Agrarian Synthesis." See *Jesse Stuart: Essays on His Work*, ed. J. R. LeMaster and Mary Washington Clarke (Lexington, Kentucky, 1977).

> In deed and word he shows himself
> A chip of the old block.

> In youth, 'tis said, he liked not school—
> Of tasks he was no lover;
> He wrote sums in a ciphering book,
> Which had a pasteboard cover.[15]

Notwithstanding, by the summer of 1850, when Whitman's poem "Resurgemus" was published in the New York *Tribune*, he had found his new direction. From that point on he came to eschew traditional prosody and increasingly cultivated his free verse techniques. There were occasional regressions to the traditions of his early verse—for example, "O Captain! My Captain!," "Dirge for Two Veterans," and "Pioneers! O Pioneers!"—but he would abandon those to become the champion of the new American prosody as well as the poet of the new American sensibility. Whitman did not spend his days worrying about the past; his vision was of the future. In Victorian England the break with tradition came largely through the work of such groups as the Pre-Raphaelites, the Aesthetes, and Decadents, but in America it came through Walt Whitman.

With a new system of versification or prosody comes a new system of everything else characterizing the poet's task, and for Whitman the system itself corresponds to a new way of looking at the world, a different way of getting at experience—all of which amounts to raising questions about sensibility, about what it is and how it is shaped, and about how that shaping makes a personal as well as a national difference. Even though one may not accept T. S. Eliot's timing for what he calls "dissociation of sensibility," the idea is not easily dismissed. The fact is that something similar to what Eliot describes has happened. Both the American Revolution and the French Revolution came near the end of the eighteenth

---

15. For the entire poem see *The Collected Writings of Walt Whitman* (New York, 1963), VI, 3-4. Edited by Thomas L. Brasher, this volume is entitled *The Early Poems and the Fiction*.

century, and both stand as reminders that an old way of life was on its way out. Monarchy and absolute rule would be replaced by democracy and representative government. The Industrial Revolution, which began in England around the middle of the eighteenth century, contributed significantly to such change. With the death of monarchy, of course, came the death of monarchaic sensibility. A medieval hierarchy of order fell, the evidence of which is most observable in what happened to established religion. In art, the fall meant the death of old forms with, for the most part, nothing to take their place.

Whitman perceived the relationship between style in government and form in art. He became the great poet of democracy and, like Matthew Arnold, for whom he apparently had little regard, viewed art as an extension of life, as a means for shaping and modifying sensibility. Throughout the prefaces and the essays one finds Whitman voicing his democratic idealism, as he does throughout his poems. "Song of Myself" (1855) is the poet's greatest celebration of sensibility in the new world, and as such it is his greatest achievement as poet of democracy. In *Leaves of Grass*, his subject is the emergence of a new sensibility—a fact which has not been given as much attention as it deserves in Whitman scholarship.

In order to appreciate fully how moral Stuart's vision of art and life is one needs a definition of the new sensibility, and for Whitman's time one of the best definitions is to be found in the conclusion to Walter Pater's *Renaissance*. Concerning the function of art, writes Pater: "Not the fruit of experience, but experience itself, is the end. A counted number of pulses only is given to us of a variegated, dramatic, life. How may we see in them all that is to be seen in them by the finest senses?"[16] The quality of life, contends Pater, lies in passion, in "expanding that interval" called life by accelerating one's pulsations or sensations, not in longevity. Pater's definition of the new sensibility is not far removed from that being celebrated by Whitman.

16. Reprinted in *Selections from Walter Pater*, ed. Edward Everett Hale, Jr. (New York, 1901), pp. 21-22.

In our own time one can look to Susan Sontag for a defini-
tion and find that it is remarkably like Pater's. In her essay
entitled "The One Culture and the New Sensibility" Sontag
sets out to refute the old idea of two cultures found in the writ-
ings of such people as C. P. Snow and Van Wyck Brooks. Deny-
ing anything resembling a conflict of cultures, she asserts
that what we are witnessing is the creation of a new kind of
sensibility. Furthermore, as she sees it the new sensibility is
rooted in experiences which are new in the history of the
human race. Among these new experiences she lists extremes
in social and physical mobility, crowdedness and un-
availability of land, proliferation of mass-produced com-
modities, mass production of art objects, and the availability
of new sensations through physical speed as well as the speed
of images through mass media.

Because of these new experiences, according to Sontag,
the function of art is being transformed. Rather than existing
as an instrument for depicting and commenting on secular
reality, or as an instrument for promoting religious or moral
causes, today art "is a new kind of instrument, an instrument
for modifying consciousness and organizing new modes of
sensibility."[17] For Sontag, as well as for Pater, experience is
not the means to anything; it is the end, and the quality of
sensation or pulsation is the measure of experience. For both,
art is not moral; it is amoral, and the new sensibility is
amoral. To Sontag and Pater, whether we live in an ordered
universe makes no difference. The idea is totally irrelevant to
art and to life.

Jesse Stuart is aware that what Susan Sontag says about
modern culture is true, but he cannot accept it. Inherent in his
refusal to accept modern cultural values is a refusal to accept
the modern sensibility, and inherent in that is a refusal to
accept modern art. In the Ransom-Tate controversy over
Eliot's *Waste Land* Stuart is obviously on the side of Ransom.
When confronted with the issue, he simply contends that he
has not changed his beliefs about man and the universe. Nor

17. *Against Interpretation* (New York, 1966), p. 296.

has he changed them about art: "I follow my own feelings, my own heart beats, my own impulse on these matters. So much depends on subject matter and how we feel."[18] His almost exclusive use of the sonnet as form stands as the most convincing evidence of his refusal to accept a rapidly changing American culture along with the art produced by that culture. He continued to insist on the art forms of an hierarchical or authoritarian society—forms which might have been appropriate in an antebellum agricultural South.

The opposing directions in which Whitman and Stuart developed should be quite clear. Whitman, born into the old European tradition in America, reveled in the prospects of the new sensibility and actively cultivated it in his art. In a large measure he predicted the future of American culture. In addition to celebrating the man at the plow, he celebrated America's teeming cities, commerce, and industry. By contrast, Stuart was born at the time American life and art were in great transition—the time at which the old European tradition was disappearing. The expatriot movement associated with World War I stands as a reminder of that fact. After Vanderbilt, with an ideology reinforced by the Fugitives and the Agrarians, Stuart chose the opposite direction. He chose to reclaim the past in order to salvage the future. He chose to avoid the decadence associated with industry and commerce in America's cities in favor of life on the land. And even though he never belonged to the Agrarian Movement, the years have proved him to be the most constant Agrarian of them all.

When one is knowledgeable about the extent of Jesse Stuart's Fugitive-Agrarian orientation, when one is knowledgeable about the writer's vision concerning the future of America, he is then in a position to make a valid assessment of Stuart's place in American letters. Only then can he appreciate what Bird meant when he referred to Stuart as an anachronism, and only then can he see the foolishness of ap-

---

18. Letter to the writer, January 19, 1968.

plying criteria of open form to a poet of closed or received form. To perform such an exercise is obviously to do a grave injustice to both.

As far as the chronicle is concerned, it has been valuable in carrying out Stuart's purpose. Through using the chronicle he has held before the American public an alternative to the industrial state, firmly convinced that the good life exists nowhere outside a right relationship with the soil. He chose Eastern Kentucky as the area to be chronicled not only because he lived there and knew the area, but because the pioneer spirit seemed to remain there long after it had disappeared from most of the country. Super highways came to Appalachia later than they did to most other places. Industry came later, and Appalachian poverty programs conducted over the years remind us that the population has always been denied the level of prosperity shared by other Americans. As an isolated and underdeveloped area, Appalachia lends itself well to such a chronicle, but much of the mystery once associated with the word "Appalachia" has disappeared because of our access to the area by road, by plane, and by television camera.

The effect which the modernization of Appalachia has had on the chronicle is to render it ineffectual and unconvincing for the outsider. There is little point in recording a way of life like that of the remainder of Americans, a problem which Stuart has tried to resolve in a number of ways. Largely for artistic purposes, he has ignored the modernization and has concentrated heavily on writing about his farm as well as the immediately adjacent area. Also, the chronicle has continued to grow because of Stuart's memory of what once was rather than his acknowledgment of what is. Memory and imagination often bring ambience of the past to bear upon a present situation, and when the incident is written into the chronicle that ambience remains. Frequently, however, ambience and incident are both from the past, and the present is ignored altogether. Such is the nature of the chronicle, a nature which directly concerns problems of being a regional writer, a popular writer.

One must admit from the outset that Jesse Stuart is a regional writer, at least in the general sense that he has chosen to write about a region. To a large extent he is regional in another sense—he writes not only about but for a region. In an essay entitled "The Regional Motive" Wendell Berry identifies two forms of regionalism which he finds distasteful. There is a regionalism, he contends, which "behaves like nationalism,"[19] and there is one based upon condescension, behaving like an exploitive industry offering for sale the quaintnesses, eccentricities, and picturesqueness of a region to outsiders. Both varieties, according to Berry, dangerously generalize and stereotype the life of a region. Both impose false literary and cultural generalizations upon the region. One can find numerous examples of both varieties in Stuart's poetry and fiction, but he can find far more of what Berry endorses as substantial regionalism.

For Berry, substantial regionalism is simply defined as "*local life aware of itself.* It would tend to substitute for the myths and stereotypes of a region a particular knowledge of the life of the *place* one lives in and intends to *continue* to live in. It pertains to living as much as to writing, and it pertains to living *before* it pertains to writing."[20] Berry sounds very much like Stuart concerning man's relationship to the land: "The health and even the continuance of our life in America, in all regions, require that we enact in the most particular terms a responsible relationship to our land. For that reason the agrarianism of the Southern Agrarians was, in my opinion, a beginning that promised something in the way of a cure."[21] Without a complex knowledge of one's place or locale, continues Berry, and without faithfulness to that place, it will be used carelessly and eventually rendered uninhabitable. By extension, the explanation also applies to the culture of a country. When the culture becomes no more than super-

---

19. For Berry's discussion see *Southern Review* 6 (1970), 972-977.
20. *Ibid.*, p. 975.
21. *Ibid.*, p. 974.

ficial and decorative, the very survival of that culture is endangered.

Quoting Thomas Hardy, Berry argues that continuity of environment is essential to survival. Continuity of environment supposes continuity of information—names, stories, and relics—held in the collective memory of those who inhabit a place. Through memory and association, continues Berry, the land is made fit for human habitation and men are made fit to be the inhabitants. The observation sounds very like what Robert Penn Warren means when he refers to what he calls the "death of history." Whatever a place means to its inhabitants, that meaning is not a "thing-in-itself." Such meaning has a history, a history recorded in memory and old association.

This is the point at which Jesse Stuart as chronicler is at his best. Because of his Agrarian (and agrarian) stance, and his vision concerning the future of America, he has spent a lifetime examining the past. Through book after book he has made the history of his area available for new generations of readers. His history of Appalachian culture will be of importance to the nation's cultural historians for a long time to come, and those who set out to write a new history of Appalachian culture will find him indispensable. But widespread national acceptance of Stuart, elevating him to the status of a major American writer, supposes radical changes in the American sensibility. It supposes the collapse of our large cities, the collapse of industry, the failure of technology, and in general the demise of what the Agrarians referred to as the applied sciences. Such catastrophe would throw great masses of people back to an intimate relationship with the land, but it would also mean the death of one of the world's great civilizations. In times of crisis cultures change, but there is no such thing in cultural change as recapturing a former time. The American sensibility can never again meet expectations of the Agrarian Movement; we may be on a crash course toward total destruction, but there is no going back.

Contending that what he calls "urban nomadism" could

only have happened as a result of monumental errors in land use, economics, and intellectual pursuit, Berry states the alternatives as he sees them:

> With the urbanization of the country so nearly complete, it may seem futile to the point of madness to pursue an ethic and a way of life based upon devotion to a place and devotion to the land. And yet I do pursue such an ethic and such a way of life, for I believe they hold the only possibility, not just for a decent life, but for survival. And the two concerns—decency and survival—are *not* separate, but are intimately related. For as the history of agriculture in the Orient very strongly suggests, it is not the life that is fittest (that is to say, the most violent) that survives, but rather the life that is most decent—the life that is most generous and wise in its relation to the earth.[22]

The passage could have been written by Stuart; it states his sentiments exactly. It also supposes that the city has not become a natural habitat for modern man, although it does not preclude the idea that man could be made to feel at home there. If such a thing happened, it is conceivable that devotion to that place and that land could produce the decency which Berry considers necessary for survival.

Chapter 3 considers some of Stuart's early faults as a writer, including faults in technique. Some of those faults have stayed with him, and the extent to which they have marks him as an inferior poet. Regardless of his vision or his predilection for old forms, using a word whose sense is not appropriate to the context merely for the sake of completing a rhyme is bad technique. Padding a line solely for the sake of syllable count is likewise bad technique. These are heinous crimes against the craft. There are also errors in judgment, such as the poet's intensive cultivation of the sonnet form. Accusations made early in Stuart's career that all of his poems sounded the same should have made him aware of that. As

---

22. *Ibid.*, p. 977.

with any other formula, that one, repeated hundreds of times, becomes boring regardless of what in the way of experience is being formulated. Having the same syllable count in the line and rhymes in the same places for hundreds of lines produces tedium. Because the images come largely from experience in one geographical area, they, too, have a high degree of similarity and sometimes become greatly redundant. Although the form or the regional images might be more tolerated one at a time, together they point up a definite error in judgment on the part of the poet.

Finally, Chapter 3 also discusses the problem of idiom that characterizes the juvenilia, a problem which has persisted throughout the poet's career. Assuming that Mary Washington Clarke is correct in her observation that Stuart is faithful to the speech of his region, the implications of such faithfulness are twofold and bear directly upon the nature of his reading audience. To his Appalachian readers, his use of idiom may be a very effective means of making "local life aware of itself," in Berry's terms. The history of a place is also the history of the speech of that place. On the other hand, for his readers beyond Appalachia his use of idiom may amount to no more than what Berry calls exploitive regionalism. That is, it may impress the outsider as characteristic of post-Civil War local color—the worst possible kind of exploitive regionalism.

Related to the idea of idiom and audience there is a long-standing, general acceptance of Stuart as a popular writer rather than an academic one, and again the evidence seems clear. The fact that his poems first appear in such publications as *Ladies' Home Journal* and *American Forests* as well as in the "little magazines" substantially bears out the case. Furthermore, the fact that his books—listed in trade journals—sell in department store book stalls instead of university bookstores adds weight to such an observation. "The particular concern of the private artist," contends Barry Ulanov, "is to distinguish himself from the mob. Everything about him is directed to special concerns, special languages, special textures, a special audience."[23] By contrast, continues Ulanov, the popular artist is very differently motivated: "Everything about him—his interests, his skills, his special gifts—leads him to box-office returns, to the largest possible audience for his work. He must become a best seller; his programs must achieve a high rating; he must find a response from the millions, or at least the hundreds of thousands, or fail to survive."[24]

When the Agrarians left Vanderbilt and took jobs in Northern universities they did it out of necessity. Had they stayed at Vanderbilt in an effort to convert their philosophy to practice, they too would have had to appeal to the masses. In short, accepting the futility of the effort, they chose to abandon it in favor of becoming private artists, in Ulanov's sense. Jesse Stuart must be viewed in the same context. But he chose the masses—chose to hold before them his model for the future of America. He is the first to admit that he has failed, but in no way does he regret having tried. He often says that life is more important than art, and that a man's apparent failures may come to be viewed quite differently at another time, and perhaps in another place. His judgments appear to have been shortsighted at times, but he has doggedly refused to alter his art or his vision. One must admire his purpose, and his determination. As for successes and failures, he may be correct. It is presently hard to conceive of his becoming a total failure. At the same time, given continued critical attention and an adequate editing of his work, another time (and perhaps another place) might find him to be of much more value than we have ever dreamed.

---

23. *The Two Worlds of American Art: The Private and the Popular* (New York, 1965), p. 11.
24. *Ibid.*

Bibliography
Index

Selected Bibliography

WORKS BY JESSE STUART:

"Album of Destiny." *Literary America* 2 (1935): 490-492.

Album of Destiny. New York: E. P. Dutton and Company, 1944.

"America's Last Carbon Copy." *Saturday Review* 40 (December 28, 1957): 5-7.

"Appalachian Suicide." *Esquire* 72 (December 1969): 104.

"Ascension of Autumn: A Rhapsody." *Southern Literary Messenger* 1 (January 1939): 16-27.

"Autobiographical Reminiscence." *University of Kansas City Review* 27 (October 1960): 57-64.

"Ballad of John Winslow." *Hawk and Whippoorwill* 1 (Spring 1960): 5-7.

Beyond Dark Hills. New York: E. P. Dutton and Company, 1938.

Come Gentle Spring. New York: McGraw-Hill Book Company, 1969.

Daughter of the Legend. New York: McGraw-Hill Book Company, 1965.

Dawn of Remembered Spring. New York: McGraw-Hill Book Company, 1972.

"Delos by the Sea." *Cincinnati Pictorial Enquirer*, May 21, 1967.

"Dry Wind of Ephesus." *Arizona Quarterly* 25 (1969): 347-348.

God's Oddling. New York: McGraw-Hill Book Company, 1960.

Harvest of Youth. Howe, Oklahoma: The Scroll Press, 1930.

Hold April. New York: McGraw-Hill Book Company, 1962.

"How Like the Great Greek God Apollo Is Our Leader." *Esquire* 64 (December 1965): 242.

Kentucky Is My Land. New York: E. P. Dutton and Company, 1952.

"Korea to the World." *Korea Journal* 3 (July 1963): 13.

The Land Beyond the River. New York: McGraw-Hill Book Company, 1973.

"Lincoln Weeps." *The Angels* 5 (Spring-Summer 1968): 5.

"Lovesong for Over Forty." *South* 3 (Fall 1970): 9-16.

"Love-Vine." *The University Review* 32 (1966): 218.

Man with a Bull-Tongue Plow. New York: E. P. Dutton and Company, 1934.

"Meeting Mr. New England, America's Greatest Poet." *Educational Forum* 23 (1959): 291-292.

"Memory Albums." *Tennessee Teacher* 37 (February 1970): 9.

"Memory Practices." *Kappa Delta Pi Record* 8 (April 1972): 112-113.

My Land Has a Voice. New York: McGraw-Hill Book Company, 1966.

My World. Lexington, Kentucky: University Press of Kentucky, 1975.

"A Poem Is Born." *South* 3 (Fall 1970): 3-8.

"Sandburg, My Hero." *Lincoln Herald* 70 (Spring 1968): 40-43.

The Seasons of Jesse Stuart: An Autobiography in Poetry, ed. Wanda Hicks. Danbury, Connecticut: Archer Editions Press, 1976.

"Shinglemill Symphony." *American Forests* 71 (December 1965): 28-29.

Taps for Private Tussie. New York: E. P. Dutton and Company, 1943.

"Three Teachers and a Book." In *Pages*, edited by Matthew J. Bruccoli, pp. 90-103. Detroit: Gale Research Company, 1976.

To Teach, To Love. New York: World Publishing Company, 1970.

"When Not to Take Advice." *Saturday Review of Literature*, February 17, 1945, p. 11.

"Where Angry Winds Blow." *Poet Lore* 63 (Spring 1968): 29.

"Where April Sings." *Snowy Egret* 31 (Spring 1967): 21.

"Where Pindar Lived." *Caravel: A Magazine of Verse*, No. 14 (Fall 1965): 33. No volume number given.

"Why I Think *Album* Is My Best." *Prairie Schooner* 30 (1956): 32-37.

The World of Jesse Stuart: Selected Poems, ed. and with an Introduction by J. R. LeMaster. New York: McGraw-Hill Book Company, 1975.

The Year of My Rebirth. New York: McGraw-Hill Book Company, 1956.

All unpublished poems, including those from the manuscript entitled "Birdland's Golden Age," have been cited as completely as possible in my notes.

WORKS BY OTHERS:

Allen, Gay Wilson. *American Prosody*. New York: Octagon Books, 1966. Originally published in 1935 by American Book Company.

_____. *Walt Whitman Handbook*. New York: Hendricks House, 1946.

Baugh, Albert C. *A History of the English Language*. 2nd ed. New York: Appleton-Century-Crofts, 1957.

Berry, Wendell. "The Regional Motive." *Southern Review* 6 (1970): 972-977.

Bird, John. "My Friend Jesse Stuart." *Saturday Evening Post*, July 25, 1959, pp. 32-33, 79, 81-83.

Blair, Everetta Love. *Jesse Stuart: His Life and Works*. Columbia, South Carolina: University of South Carolina Press, 1967.

Browning, Sister Mary Carmel. *Kentucky Authors: A History of Kentucky Literature*. Evansville, Indiana: Keller-Crescent Company, 1968.

Carlyle, Thomas. *Critical and Miscellaneous Essays*. 2 vols. Illustrated Sterling ed. Boston: Dana Estes and Company, 1869.

Cash, W. J. *The Mind of the South*. New York: Alfred A. Knopf, 1941.

Chari, V. K. *Whitman in the Light of Vedantic Mysticism*. Lincoln, Nebraska: University of Nebraska Press, 1964.

Christman, Henry. [review] *Knickerbocker Press*, October 4, 1934. Title of review and page number not given. Found in Stuart's scrapbooks, #2, p. 13.

Clarke, Mary Washington. *Jesse Stuart's Kentucky*. New York: McGraw-Hill Book Company, 1968.

Coleridge, Samuel Taylor. *Essays and Lectures on Shakespeare and Some Other Old Poets and Dramatists*. London: Everyman Library, n.d.

_____. "On Poesy or Art." *Modern Criticism: Theory and Practice,* edited by Walter Sutton and Richard Foster, pp. 36-41. New York: The Odyssey Press, 1963.

Core, George, ed. *Southern Fiction Today*. Athens, Georgia: University of Georgia Press, 1969.

Cowan, Louise. *The Fugitive Group: A Literary History*. Baton Rouge, Louisiana: Louisiana State University Press, 1959.

Cowley, Malcolm. "Man with a Hoe." *The New Republic* 80 (1934): 342-343.

Cruttwell, Patrick. *The English Sonnet*. London: Longmans, Green and Company, 1966.

Cunningham, J. V., ed. *The Problem of Style*. Greenwich, Connecticut: Fawcett Publications, 1966.

Duffy, John. [review] *Commonweal* 40 (1944); 169. Title of review not given. Found in Stuart's scrapbooks, #15, p. 10.

Eliot, T. S. *On Poetry and Poets*. New York: Farrar, Straus and Cudahy, 1957.

Emerson, Ralph Waldo. *The Complete Works*. 12 vols. Riverside ed. Boston: Houghton, Mifflin and Company, 1844.

Engle, Paul. "Over the Mountain." *The New York Times*, September 1, 1963, sec. 7, p. 5.

Fletcher, John Gould. "Kentucky Georgics." *Poetry: A Magazine of Verse* 45 (1935): 217-220.

Foster, Ruel E. *Jesse Stuart*. Twayne Publishers, 1968.

_____. "Jesse Stuart, Short Story Writer." *Reality and Myth: Essays in American Literature*, edited by William E. Walker and Robert L. Welker, pp. 145-160. Nashville, Tennessee: Vanderbilt University Press, 1964.

Fussell, Paul, Jr. *Poetic Meter and Poetic Form*. New York: Random House, 1965.

Gross, Harvey, ed. *The Structure of Verse: Modern Essays on Prosody*, Greenwich, Connecticut: Fawcett Publications, 1966.

Hale, Edward Everett, Jr., ed. *Selections from Walter Pater*. New York: Holt Publishing Company, 1901.

Hall, Wade. *The Truth Is Funny: A Study of Jesse Stuart's Humor*. Terre Haute, Indiana: Indiana Council of Teachers of English, 1970.

Hillyer, Robert. *First Principles of Verse*. Rev. ed. Boston: The Writer, 1950.

I'll Take My Stand. Introduction to the Torchbook Edition by Louis D. Rubin, Jr. New York: Harper and Brothers, 1962.

Johns, Orrick. [review] "Book-of-the-Month Club News," ed. Harry Scherman. Title and date not given. Found in Stuart's scrapbooks, dated 1934-1935, p. 9.

Kohler, Dayton. "Jesse Stuart and James Still, Mountain Regionalists." *College English* 3 (1942): 523-533.

Lanz, Henry. *The Physical Basis of Rime*. Stanford, California: Stanford University, 1931.

Leavell, Frank Hartwell. "The Literary Career of Jesse Stuart." Unpublished Ph.D. dissertation, Vanderbilt University, 1965.

LeMaster, J. R. and Mary Washington Clarke, eds. *Jesse Stuart: Essays on His Work*. Lexington, Kentucky: University Press of Kentucky, 1977.

MacLeish, Archibald. *Poetry and Experience*. Cambridge: Riverside Press, 1960.

Mims, Edwin. [review in Nashville paper] Title, name of paper, and date not given. Found in Stuart's scrapbooks, #2, p. 22.

Pennington, Lee. *The Dark Hills of Jesse Stuart*. Cincinnati: Harvest Press, 1967.

Perry, Dick. *Reflections of Jesse Stuart*. McGraw-Hill Book Company, 1971.

Ramey, Lee Oly. "An Inquiry into the Life of Jesse Stuart as Related to His Literary Development and a Critical Study of His Works." Unpublished M.A. thesis, Ohio University, 1941.

Ransom, John Crowe. *The World's Body*. Port Washington, New York: Kennikat Press, 1964. This edition published by arrangement with Charles Scribner's Sons.

Sandburg, Carl. *Complete Poems*. New York: Harcourt, Brace, 1950.

Smith, C. Alphonso. *Repetition and Parallelism in English Verse*. New York: University Publishing Company, 1894.

Snyder, Richard and Robert McGovern, eds. *Read Out, Read In.* Ashland, Ohio: Ashland Poetry Press, 1971.

Sontag, Susan. *Against Interpretation.* New York: Farrar, Straus, and Giroux, 1966.

Sullivan, Walter. "Southern Writers in the Modern World: Death by Melancholy." *Southern Review* 6 (1970): 907-919.

Tate, Allen. *Poems.* New York: Charles Scribner's Sons, 1960.

Ulanov, Barry. *The Two Worlds of American Art: The Private and the Popular.* New York: The Macmillan Company, 1965.

Wagner, Linda Welshimer. *The Poems of William Carlos Williams.* Middletown, Connecticut: Wesleyan University Press, 1964.

Wellek, Rene and Austin Warren. *Theory of Literature.* 3rd ed. New York: Harcourt, Brace and World, 1956.

Westerfield, Hargis. "*Harvest of Youth:* Jesse Stuart's First Published Book." *American Book Collector* 13 (February 1963): 23-24.

Wheelwright, Philip. *Metaphor and Reality.* Bloomington, Indiana: Indiana University Press, 1962.

Whitman, Walt. *The Collected Writings.* 8 vols. New York: New York University Press, 1963.

_____. *Complete Poetry and Prose.* 2 vols. New York: Pellegrini and Cudahy, 1948. This is the Deathbed Edition containing Malcolm Cowley's famous Introduction. Reprinted by Garden City Books in 1954.

_____. *Notes and Fragments*, ed. Richard M. Bucke. London: Ontario: Printed for the editor, 1899. Republished in *The Complete Writings of Walt Whitman*, IX.

_____. *Pictures.* edited by Emory Holloway. London: Faber and Gwyer, 1927.

Winters, Yvor. *The Function of Criticism.* 2nd ed. Denver: Alan Swallow Press, 1957.

Woodbridge, Hensley C. *Jesse and Jane Stuart: A Bibliography.* 2nd ed. Murray, Kentucky: Murray State University, 1969.

Index

Fictional characters are in boldface.